TELL ME, FRIENDS

TELL ME, FRIENDS:

Contemporary Stories
and Plays of Tanzania

by Students and Staff at the University of Dar es Salaam

edited by Lilian Osaki
and Lisa María B. Noudéhou

Mkuki na Nyota Publishers Ltd
P. O. Box 4246
Dar es Salaam
www.mkukinanyota.com

Published by:
Mkuki na Nyota Publishers Ltd
P. O. Box 4246
Dar es Salaam
Email: contact@mkukinanyota.com
www.mkukinanyota.com

Edited by: Lilian Osaki and Lisa María B. Noudéhou

First Edition, 2009

ISBN 978-9987-08-048-9

Contents

Introduction

This third collection of *Tell Me, Friends* brings together stories and plays written by students and staff at the University of Dar es Salaam between 2006 and 2008. The main objective of this publication is to promote creative writing, both the writing itself and the enjoyment therein.

When reviewing the submissions for the collection, we found that these contemporary narratives are strongly engaged in addressing social problems. Thus, we would like to say a few words about literature and society.

Literature (we teachers of literature agree) is more satisfying than just any text. We don't read the telephone directory or a dictionary from front to back; we usually skim through a newspaper or a trade journal. Such texts are usually just words on paper, but literature requires the thoughtful union of word, thought, and form. Inspiration and careful work produce texts that are objects of art, that are philosophical meditations, that are … somehow more than ordinary texts … and these texts, we call literature.

This literature has different kinds of relationships with readers. As propaganda, the text, in its most pejorative form, seeks to control readers, defining the world and doing the thinking for the reader. As didactic literature, the text teaches, providing guidelines for the reader. John Bunyan's *The Pilgrim's Progress*, for example, uses the main character to chart the spiritual progress required of a Christian, while Shaban Robert's *Utubora Mkulima* provides a farmer as a role model for good behavior and his *Kufikirika* illustrates good governance through an allegorical country and its leaders. As literature in its most essential form, the text fully entertains the reader and asks difficult philosophical and social questions, without providing wholly definitive answers, all through the most beautifully chosen words. A text can thus seek to order, teach, or challenge its readers.

In Africa, we turn to orature for our first examples of such carefully crafted language. The *griot*, the *ngoma*, traditionally played the role of historian and social commentator in addition to that of poet and singer. Inherent to the role was both the act of reflecting the society and of providing critical observations about the people therein. The genre of the praise poem, for example, catalogues events and praises the person addressed, but also comments on action and character, offering guidance to the listeners. In the twentieth century transition from colony to independent nation, the authors of written works carried on this role of the *griot*. Their essays, histories, stories, novels, plays, and poetry generally supported national independence, providing criticism of the colonial society and imagining a new, independent society. Today, contemporary African authors generally perceive their own roles as crucial to the success of their communities.

The authors across the continent who have reflected on their roles are many. They include Ugandan, Okot p'Bitek, Kenyan, Ngugi wa Thiong'o, and South African, Nadine Gordimer. p'Bitek, in his essay "Artist, the Ruler" (1986), argues that "the artist creates the central ideas around which other leaders, law makers, chiefs, judges, heads of clans, family heads, construct and sustain social institutions. But more, they also compose the festivals in which these ideas are celebrated" (39). He goes on to stress that "in any society, anywhere, in any age, there are two types of rulers: namely, the artist who provides and sustains the fundamental ideas, the foundation of society; and the political chieftain, who comes to power with the aid of his soldier and rich business brethren, who merely puts these ideas into practice in ruling or misruling society" (39). For p'Bitek, the author is clearly a leader of society. Also formulated in the 1980s, Ngugi's well known argument for the need to write in African languages, instead of in the colonial European languages, is based on the assumption that the role of the writer in Africa is, in part, to counter colonialism and neo-colonialism. In other words, he argues that the expression of specific African cultures and personhoods in literature addresses the alienation suffered by Africans. Gordimer argues for a similarly socially situated role for the author in her Nobel Prize Lecture of 1991: she writes that as authors in general, "we spend our lives attempting to interpret through the word the readings we take in the societies, the world of which we are part. It is in this sense, this inextricable, ineffable participation, that writing is always and at once an exploration of self and of the world; of individual and collective being" (196), an effort whose objective, she goes on to say, is the pursuit of truths about this state of being. In a later lecture, she considers the obstacles facing African authors in the 21st century and concludes that in response to censorship, authors must "ensure that our implicit role—supplying a critique of society for the greater understanding and enrichment of life there—will be respected" (35), and that in response to the globalization of pulp television, "literature in Africa not only has to express the lives of the people but also has to assert the beauty and interest of this reality against mega-subculture— the new opium of the people..." (36). The writer, for Gordimer, thus plays a complex role as a member of society, a supporter of the cultural expression of the society, and a commentator on the same society. All three authors view writers as being situated in and responsible to particular societies.

In Tanzania, President Julius Nyerere set the tone for Tanzanians through the expectation that all people have the responsibility "to improve the well-being of the community to which we belong" (last paragraph of the 1970 speech, "Education for Service and not for Selfishness"). Such an expectation requires authors to be socially engaged. Dramatist Penina Muhando Mlama, for example, takes such social engagement seriously. She notes in 1974 (in the years after the Arusha Declaration), "I think when I do my writing I want to pick any problem which is troubling the people in Tanzania at the present time. Because I see myself as having a duty to try to help the society either in showing where the problems are or trying to suggest solutions to problems or at least to make the people aware that the sources of this and that problem are in this and that thing" (140). She says some ten years later that, "Many African writers now find it more difficult than ever before not to say something about the pathetic situation of African people. ... The writer often chooses to announce her or his position, or to conscientize and to mobilize his or her audience into understanding, analyzing their plight. Even though the situation seems to be so hopeless, the writer feels the need to tell the audience not to despair, and the bolder writer exhorts them to stand up and fight" (298). She further defines the social role as one in which "the African writer is the man or woman of culture, one who preserves, rejuvenates, and guides his or her society's perception of an acceptable way of life, its morals, values and attitudes, its integrity and identity,...(300).

As outlined by the scholar Farouk Topan, Tanzanian authors such as Shaaban Robert, Mung'ong'o, and Ruhumbika have written novels that evaluate contemporary policies and look to both the past and the future in an effort to provide guidance on how better to develop a strong and peaceful Tanzania. To this list, we might add most published Tanzanian authors, from Prince Kagwema to our contemporaries, Elieshi Lema and Abdulrazak Gurnah. Topan also quotes the author Saad S. Yahya, as defining the writer's motivation: Saad writes that his own collection of stories was "born out of pain – the pain of seeing the African in the situation he is today years after independence, the pain of not daring to act and do what one ought to do, the pain of participating in the experiment of developing Swahili and seeing to it that it is accorded the status due to it, the pain of imagining the Africa of tomorrow" (118). His emphasis is on empathy with his fellows and participation in the society. It is clear that Tanzanian authors, like their African colleagues, view authors as being situated in and responsible to their people.

Thus, we can conclude that authors in Africa understand their role as one in which they speak on behalf of and to the societies in which they live; we can further conclude that a literature which is engaged in addressing social problems is actually the norm, not the exception, in Tanzania.

Overview of the Stories:

"Our Man" by Saida Yahya-Othman is a story about two old friends, Seif and Ali, who spend most of their afternoons at a rendezvous called "Talking corner." Being of middle age, their talk centers around the state of the world today, but also includes occasional recollections of the bad times when people of the Island of Zanzibar suffered. The suffering is narrated by Ali who, unlike most of his friends, never left the islands. The man who is responsible for the gravest brutality is at the heart of a revelation which takes Seif completely by surprise.

"The Window Seat" by Benjamin Branoff tells a humorous story of a young man, a foreigner, who boards a *daladala* from Mlimani via Mwenge to the postal office down town. The foreigner meets many people who squeeze themselves in the small bus, including a beautiful Tanzanian girl who touches the behind of the foreigner. This will be one bus ride the young man will never forget!

"The Concealed Project" by Zuhura Badru tells of a bogus project that is funded by a reputable organization that manages to secure funds from a rich western country. The story reveals the secrets of how Non Governmental Organizations collude with local leaders to embezzle funds donated for development projects in the rural areas and focuses on a woman who tries to stand strong and remain honest.

"The Total Crisis" by Simon Mlundi is a sad story about an innocent boy who finds himself expelled from school without committing any crime, a boy who must go through hell looking for justice. As the saying goes "justice delayed is justice denied" and so the boy suffers through different hands, including those of his best friend, as he seeks to re-enroll in school.

"Testimony" by Emmanuel Lema is the last story in our collection. Written in a flashback the narrative tells a story of a young ambitious girl called Nsia. This beautiful girl's life is destroyed by a government official who rapes and abandons her. Nsia, in turn, abandons the baby boy she cannot support, and goes to town where she works as a bar maid and prostitute. The story follows her difficulties and those of a daughter she gives birth to in town.

Overview of the Plays:

"The Monster" by Anna Chikoti tells the story of how individuals are being threatened by an unknown menace, and of how the community attempts to combat the 'Monster' behind the suffering and deaths.

"Love is…" by Kimberley McLeod is set in the home of an African-American family in Savannah, Georgia in the United States of America. Although it is Thanksgiving, which is a time for celebration and thankfulness, the devout Christian parents soon find themselves in direct conflict with their visiting son and his fiancée.

"A Tanzanian Rooftop" by Benjamin Branoff is set on the rooftop of an international dormitory in Dar es Salaam. The setting allows the characters, both local and exchange students, to survey the world around them and to offer commentary on such various subjects as love, the experience of visiting Tanzania for the first time, violence, and student unrest.

"Judges on Trial" by Frowin Paul Nyoni takes place in a courtroom presided over by a judge who fears for his life and a clerk who tries to assert order. Excitement mounts as a ghost judge soon takes over the trial and proceeds to put the living judge on trial.

"The Route to Success" by Yunus Ng'umbi tells the story of a young man, Kigwanda, who seeks wealth and a brighter future. Instead of working in the tea factory, he chooses to follow in the steps of a childhood friend and finds quick wealth. The play explores the repercussions of this choice.

"The Mop" by Vicensia Shule takes place in the fictional country of Nyakibonga and considers very philosophical questions: What is the purpose of the mop? How should it be cared for? What is the optimum quality of a mop? The answers to these questions provide the keys to successful national development.

These collected plays and short stories reflect the social conditions of contemporary Tanzania. If we concur with New Historicists who argue that a text should be studied in relation to the historical and cultural conditions of its production, then we have to accept that "Literature does not occupy a 'trans-historical' *aesthetic* realm which is independent of the economic, social, and political conditions specific to an era" (Abrams 192). The plays and stories collected here have been formed and structured by the particular conditions of time and place. The suffering and torture experienced by Ali in "Our Man," the corruption in "The Concealed Project" or the prostitution in "Testimony" – all these are representations of the eras in which they are written. It is therefore valid to note that the stories and plays in our collection provide reading pleasure, not only to the readers who value the New Critical ideal of an artistically resolved plot, but also to those readers who value the New Historical ideal of the narrative that addresses ongoing, unresolved conflicts in our societies.

We invite you to read, enjoy, and share these stories and plays.

Lilian Osaki   Lisa María Burgess Noudéhou

Works Cited

Abrams, M.H. *A Glossary of Literary Terms*. United Kingdom: Thomson Wadsworth, 2005.

Bunyan, John. *A Pilgrim's Progress*. 1678-1684.

Gordimer, Nadine. "Writing and Being." 1991. Rpt. *Living in Hope and History: Notes from our century*. London: Bloomsbury, 1999.

Gordimer, Nadine. "Turning the Page: African Writers and the Twenty-first Century". 1992. Rpt. *Living in Hope and History: Notes from our century*. London: Bloomsbury, 1999.

Mlama, Penina. Interview of 09 September 1974. *Conversations with African Writers: Interviews with Twenty-Six African Authors*. Conducted and edited by Lee Nichols. Washington, DC: Voice of America, 1981.

Mlama, Penina Muhando. "Creating in the Mother-Tongue: The Challenges to the African Writer Today." 1990. Rpt. *Women Writing Africa: The Eastern Region*. NY: The Feminist Press, 2007.

Ngugi wa Thiong'o. *Decolonizing the Mind: The Politics of Language in African Literature*. London: James Currey, 1986.

Ngugi wa Thiong'o. "Writing against Neo-Colonialism." *Criticisms and Ideology*. Ed. K. Petersen. Uppsala: Scandinavian Institute of African Studies, 1988.

Nyerere, Julius. "Education for Service and not for Selfishness." 1970. Rpt. *Nyerere on Education: Selected Essays and Speeches 1954-1998*. Dar es Salaam: Hakielimu and E&D Limited, 2004.

p'Bitek, Okot. "Artist the Ruler." *Artist the Ruler: Essays on Art, Culture and Values*. Nairobi: Heinemann Kenya, 1986.

Robert, Shaban. *Utubora Mkulima*. 1968.

Robert, Shaban. *Kufikirika*. 1967.

Topan, Farouk. "Why Does a Swahili Writer Write? Euphoria, Pain, and Popular Aspirations in Swahili Literature." *Research in African Literatures*. 37:3, Fall 2006.

UNESCO. *The Cultural Dimension of Development*. The Hague: The Netherlands National Commission for UNESCO, 1985.

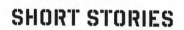

SHORT STORIES

"Our Man"

by Saida Yahya-Othman

"I'm afraid I'm a bit late. I passed by the mosque and old man Hamisi cornered me and started his usual moaning about his son-in-law. I couldn't stop him once he'd started." Seif was standing just outside the door of his friend's house while he spoke. He couldn't enter without being invited, and his friend seemed busy with the spokes of his bicycle, his body bent low in concentration. The light inside the house was not very good.

"No, no, not to worry, my friend," Ali said in an easy drawl, looking up with the smile of an expectation fulfilled. "Your lateness has given me the time to check on this old wreck of mine. I think I'll take it with me now and leave it at the mechanic's. It's not anything I can deal with."

"Can I help?" asked Seif, just being kind really, as was his wont. He didn't know the first thing about bicycles. Ali knew this well enough, and laughed. "If I can't deal with it, old friend, I can assure you only a proper mechanic can. Right, let's go."

They set off, as they did almost every afternoon, except that today Ali was dragging his bicycle alongside him. Ever since Seif had returned home from a self-imposed exile, he had gotten into the stride of his fellow islanders. Once back from work, he snatched a quick post-lunch snooze, then freshened up and went by his friend Ali's house. This was hardly ten minutes away, and along the way Seif would stop occasionally to offer *salaams* to an acquaintance, or give a few tips to children playing football, or buy himself a refreshing coconut drink. It was one of the few pleasures of his present life, this walk in the late afternoon, the heat of the sun slightly tempered by the breeze from the sea. But an even greater pleasure was the conversation he had with his friend Ali, once he had collected him from his house, on their way to their rendezvous with their friends, their Talking Corner. This was where the friends gathered in the afternoons, to have what they were all convinced were serious and weighty discussions about the state of the world. Never mind that the world for them often did not stretch beyond their tiny island. But they had an enormously good time. Occasionally one of them would have a brush with a minor scandal, in the family or at work, and then the others would tease the poor man ruthlessly, until he sneaked abjectly away, only to return the next day, when all would have been forgotten. It was all good-hearted bantering, and the members of the Corner would always be the first to come to each other's defence. Not that that was often necessary, now. There were times, though, …. Ah, but those turbulent and cruel times were past now, for good.

It was of these times that Seif spent hours talking to his friend Ali. Unlike most of the others in the Corner, who had at one time or other left the island to get some breathing space elsewhere, to escape the suffocation of the oppression and injustice, to hide in cowering fear, even, Ali had never left. He had been there to see it all – the terror, the imprisonments, the imposed famine, the torture, the deaths. Seif always wondered how Ali could have gone through all that, and still remain such a wholesome person. For except in those moments when Ali was actually recounting the horrors of his life in prison, it was difficult to see him as other than a cheerful, quiet-spoken, immensely dependable fellow. But Seif knew better. For in the years since his return, he had spent so much time with Ali that he had come to know every shifting line on his face, and the meaning of every flicker from his eyes. And he knew, in the Talking Corner sometimes, when the fellows were bellowing with laughter, or trying to outdo each other in getting their views heard, he knew why Ali's eyes would suddenly look like those of a man whom death had caught by surprise; in the middle of joy with his mates, the sudden descent of the terror from long ago, blanketing everything else.

On their daily walks to the Talking Corner, Seif and Ali always passed by the market. Though it would be late afternoon, there would always be a few vendors still left, trying to clear the now shrivelled fruits and vegetables, so they wouldn't have to offer them again to their customers come morning. As daily visitors to the market themselves, Seif and Ali knew most of the vendors, and they would shout out greetings to them, often for the second time that day. Some of the vendors had been prominent public officials who had fallen on bad times, or had been part of the constant purges of previous years, and now struggled with the only means available to make ends meet. There was one old man in particular who always greeted them with just that extra bit of warmth, often stopping whatever he was doing to exchange a few words with them. If things had been going well for the day, he would even offer them a few guavas or ripe bananas "for the children." When Seif first returned, he had been away so long that he had lost touch with who was who, and who had been what. Ali often had to fill him in, on both their old friends and the new people that Seif was meeting. Seif had once asked Ali who the friendly old vendor was, and Ali had replied, "Oh, just an old friend of mine. He's one of the fallen heroes."

"From government?" Seif had been curious.

"Yes, he was in the security service."

"I wouldn't have thought you'd have had much to do with those guys," Seif could not hide his puzzlement.

"Well, you know how it is. If there is anything that I have learnt from all that business, it is to be tolerant."

"That business," was Ali's way of referring to his seven years in prison. It was just like him to use such an innocent, neutral term for the hell that was his life during those years. Seif had felt his own hair stand on end as Ali related to him the torture "sessions" that had faced them in prison. Ali had survived. Many of his friends did not, names struck off the prison list, if there was ever one, with no announcement, no explanation, no proper burial. The "sessions" were always led by a man who the detainees had labelled "Our Man." It was a wonder that they still had the humour to do that. Our Man would visit them at least once a month, with his team of "experts," each specialised in a different facet within the "art of torture" as he called it, and each using his skills to the full. The only time Our Man would leave Ali and his mates alone was when he found them praying. He was a deeply religious man. And he did not mind waiting till they finished their prayers. Then the screams and wails would begin, to ricochet off the walls, out and down the corridors, and out, out of consciousness, thankfully. Seif had wanted to know where Our Man was now, and Ali had replied, "Oh, he must be around somewhere. He was quite a survivor."

Seif would sometimes wake up in a sweat in the middle of the night, after reliving Ali's ordeal in his dreams, and would ask himself why this was happening to him. Even as dreams, they plunged him in the depths of despair. He knew he would never rid himself of the guilt of having left his friends to suffer those horrors. "But they chose to stay," an inner voice would whisper.

"No they didn't. They had nowhere to go, and I did." Seif knew that his staying behind would not have helped his friends. One more death, or one more crippled body and soul would have done nothing to the cause. And now, now, at least, he could be here to listen to Ali, to share with him the after-pain, to understand?

The following week, a Thursday it was, Seif found Ali's front door closed when he went to collect him for their daily walk to the Talking Corner. That happened occasionally, when Ali had to do something and did not have the time to inform his friend. So Seif had to knock on the door. Ali's wife appeared, her face breaking into a smile of pleasure when she saw Seif. They sometimes had a little chat when Seif had to wait for Ali to finish something. She and Ali had been married for nearly thirty years, and she had waited and suffered with her husband during the long seven years. The experience had aged her more than it had Ali. She looked gaunt and haunted, as if not quite believing that it was finally over. But she had not lost her warmth towards others.

Ali had gone to a funeral, his wife said.

"Oh? Anyone I know?" Seif tended to be rather lax on these social callings, so Ali usually did not bother to inform him about them.

"Yes, I've heard you talk about him with Ali. It's the old fruit vendor at the market. You know, the one who gave you some of his rotten old fruit sometimes."

Rotten fruit? Seif thought that was rather unkind coming from Ali's wife, especially seeing that the man was dead.

"Oh yes! It must have been very sudden. We saw him only yesterday."

"Yes, pity," said Ali's wife, then burst into tears. Seif was now very puzzled indeed; he had never seen her so emotional before. He did not know how to respond, and felt that the few comforting words he muttered were totally inadequate. So he asked her to sit down with him on the *baraza* outside the house, and tried to calm her. Her sobs subsided after a short while, but it was clear to Seif that Ali's wife did not want to talk about her outburst. Seif had no alternative but to leave her.

He didn't see Ali till Friday prayers. When he did, he couldn't help mentioning the odd behaviour of Ali's wife the previous day. He wasn't happy with his own explanation of it, that the wife was one of those people who cried at the death of someone even remotely known to them.

Ali smiled ruefully. "I'm afraid my wife detested the man. The mention of his name was always guaranteed to bring out some unpleasant reaction from her."

"But why did she cry then?"

"She wasn't crying for him. She was crying for herself, and for me, I suppose."

"For you?"

"Well, yes. The old vendor was Our Man."

"Window Seat"

by Benjamin Branoff

At the back of the *daladala*[1] I have a window seat, but all I can see is the road and the grass and the dirt flying by. The window is too low. Or perhaps the seat is too high. My head keeps hitting the rusty ceiling of the beat up Hyatt minivan at every bump in the road. There are many bumps in the roads of Dar es Salaam. The wallet in my back pocket jabs into my butt and reminds me how much I hate wallets. This seat is too high.

I am in a sort of sitting, fetal position. My knees are wedged between my abdomen and the seat in front of me. I'm trying not to jab the guy in front of me with my knees. Surely he wouldn't care. This isn't his first time in the sardine tin. Still, I try.

About twenty-five people are riding with me in this minivan built for ten, maybe ten. In the back, four people sit in each row. There are three of these rows; that's twelve people. People in these seats are fused at the hips. When the bumps are big, these people are pulled up and down by the people on either side of them. If you have big hips, you are not liked by the other people in your row. I have big hips. My wrestling coach used to make fun of my big hips. Fortunately, I am in a window seat so I only have to bear the guilt of the person on my right.

The aisle allowing access to these rows is accessible only when one of the tiny seats in each row is lifted on its hinge. These hinges were not made with the car; they were put there for efficiency purposes by the gentleman who owns this van.

That's twelve people. In addition to these three complete rows of four, there are two half rows of two on the right of the car, opposite to the sliding door. That's sixteen people. Another backward facing row of four divides the front of the car from the back. In this row, you are watching the other sixteen passengers

---

[1] minivan used for commuter bus services

and they are all watching you. This row sits on the engine so one learns quickly not to commit to a long ride in these seats. These seats are not that cool.

That's twenty people in the back. Twenty-one people including the conductor who stands by the sliding door. With the driver and two passengers in the front seat, that's twenty-four people. Fortunately, this is not rush hour. During rush hour, four more people will stand with the conductor by the sliding door. That's twenty-eight people. Twenty-eight people in a family sized minivan built for ten. Maybe ten. Fortunately, this is not rush hour.

We stop at the gate leaving Chuo. First I hear the footsteps. Then, I see the shiny black boots of the sentry who guards the gate to school. He walks slowly along the side of the van, peering into its windows. I cannot see him do this, but I know that's what he's doing. I have seen it before. Now, I can only see his perfectly shined boots with navy blue slacks tucked in. He is checking the van for something amiss. He doesn't seem to be trying very hard. If something were amiss, I'm not sure he'd recognise it.

He stops in front of my window. I wait for him to bang on the side of the van to signal that he has found nothing amiss and that the driver may proceed. He doesn't. Briefly, I panic. What's going on? Why has he stopped? Why has he stopped here? Then I remember that I'm high and overly paranoid. I relax. Then, the man sticks his head in the window and looks up at me.

"*Mzungu,*"[2] he says, "*Mambo?*"

"*Poa,*"[3] I say with a suspicious and surprised smile.

He takes his head out of the window, bangs on the side of the van, and bellows with laughter as we ride away. Now, everyone is looking at me and smiling. I smile back. I am a cute *mzungu.*

[2] Stranger, someone not from Tanzania – usually a White person from Europe or America.

[3] Slang exchange of greetings.

The endless barrage of dust drifts in through the open window. It's an orange, clay-like dust. It's light and nimble and clever. Furtively, it finds crevices of my body where no dust has been before. It sneaks its way into the stitching of my clothes so that when I do finally return home to the comforts of my humble dorm room, I remove my shirt in one long exaggerated motion before I even reach the door and find it to be coated with a sticky consistency of sweat and dust. I could cut down on the invasion of dust by closing the window. Closing the window denies me of the breeze. The breeze liberates me of the sweat. I need the breeze. I need the window open. I hate the dust.

We stop at Mlimani City before turning onto Mandela Road where the gray dust meets the orange, clay-like dust. My row temporarily clears.

The man sitting next to me has gotten off and an old woman who was sitting in the row in front of me has moved back. I respectfully greet her and she returns the gesture, letting me know I don't have to stay on my metaphorical knees any longer. As the row fills up again and the last person squeezes in, we all fuse our hips together. We are one. There is strength in unity. Then, the bus is off again and I return my gaze out of my open window.

Through the window, the side of the road dances with the grass and dirt in a mesmerizing spell. They dance fast. The black asphalt is slick and old and wise and grabs the dirt and grass with confidence. It wears a sleek yellow pinstripe that follows its every move. The pinstripe is everything for the asphalt right now. The pinstripe is the asphalt, it defines it. Without the pinstripe, the asphalt would be just like the dirt and the grass. The dirt and the grass are clumsy and foolish and wander like children. They are young, constantly swaying with the flow of human traffic. They do not hold the wisdom of the road so obvious in its cool, elegant yet commanding dance.

I can read my location from the consistency of this dance. Occasionally, it changes. I know I have left Chuo when the grass becomes clumsy and allows the dirt to dance with the road. In Chuo, the grass and the dirt don't dance together.

When the gray dirt turns to orange clay-like dust, I have reached Mlimani City. I am still learning the downtown dance. I am still a rookie.

A few more stops down the dusty road and we are at Mwenge. We pass a mobile music stand that a man totes around on his bike with tons of CDs and a large stereo system. The music blasts through the window as we pass. Some horrible 80s music is playing.

As we pass and the music fades, I hear the shouts of the conductors in the bus stop, advertising for their *daladalas*. I am skeptical of this idea. Other than Will and Hand, who goes to a bus stand without knowing where they're going? Why are these men trying to convince people to abandon their original plans and jump on another *daladala* to another place? I am very skeptical of this idea.

The bus stops and a million feet shuffle in and out of my window view. Feet with sandals, feet with shoes, bare feet, an *mzungu*. Wait, an *mzungu*? Who? Do I know them? Damn! I can't see. Cursed seat, it's too high. Could it have been the French girl, *Le Fille*?[4] No. No way. It was definitely a girl…I think. What if it was? Damn! If it was, I would have gotten a date from her from sure. If I leave without getting a date with *Le Fille*, I'm blaming it on these seats. Cursed seats.

Le Fille is a French foreign exchange student who lives across the courtyard from my dorm room. Of course, *Le Fille* isn't her real name. I just use it to remind myself that I can speak a little French, *un peau*, and that she is a beautiful French girl who likes to drink wine and eat brie and French fries and go to topless beaches. I should be with this French girl. I am American and French women absolutely love American men. We are savage and suave and debonair all at the same time.

---

[4]   *Le garçon* is French for 'the boy', while *la fille* is French for 'the girl'.

Her real name is Monique. I pass her occasionally on campus and smile a smile that's no ordinary smile, but a special smile. This smile I conjured up just for her. She seems to accept my smile and returns the gesture. Was that a special smile from her? I can't tell. Probably just an ordinary smile. I turn as we pass and hold my smile. Take the smile, *Le Fille*. When you are through with it, I will especially conjure it up for someone else. A man only has so many smiles.

By the time I've squeezed my way out of this unbelievably packed *daladala* and have a look around for the owner of the white feet, she is gone. I can merely see the back of her head in a sea of heads, swaying with the currents of human traffic. She is too far to justify me running foolishly through the crowd shouting her name and waving my hands like a knight in shining armor. Oh well, perhaps it was not meant to be on this day. Maybe I'm just telling myself that. Maybe it's true.

I orient myself and begin to head towards the Posta buses. They are across the way, through the sea of human traffic and past the market where anything can be bought. I try to ignore the enticing shouts of the *daladala* advertisements. They're drawing me in with their relentless offers. I begin to rethink my route. Maybe I don't want to go to Posta. Maybe I want to go to Msasani or Bagamoyo even. I could have an adventure into the unknown. I could follow my heart and disappear into the African land. I could, but perhaps I shouldn't. Perhaps it was not meant to be this day.

I find the Posta buses and soon we are off again, maneuvering through the human sea. The feet are dangerously close to the now moving *daladala*. I guess they know what they're doing. I don't hear any squishing sounds or screams of pain.

After safely negotiating the sea that occupies the bus station, we have returned to the road. To the dusty road. The dusty dancing road. For now it's still the orange clay-like dust dancing with the pinstripe. Soon though, it will change. I think. Soon it will turn into roadside slash and burn. Here, people are burning rubbish and dead foliage in piles on the side of the road. The fires slowly work their way out from the pile into the surrounding grass. They are rings of fire. And it burns, burns, burns.

Various smells drift in through the cabin. Through the front window and out mine. Sometimes these smells can be pleasant. The smell of chips *mayai* is pleasant. The smell of mountain air is pleasant. The smell of the sea. Sometimes this smell is not pleasant. Sometimes the smell is rancid.

I watch the head of the front seat passenger by the window. I'm looking for any obvious warnings of an intruding aroma. I am Sherlock Holmes. I don't see any obvious signs. What will it look like? Will the man spontaneously and violently shake his head and grab his nose and turn around, yelling of the putrid incoming? Or will he casually bring his hand to his nose and do a quick squeeze-twist-swipe motion as if he's just blown a line of coke off the dashboard? I look, but it's too late. I am still a rookie.

A rancid smell fills my nostrils and I wish I could pass the excess around. It smells of the garbage and human filth and decomposition common when waste is dealt with in the easiest, most efficient manner by piling it up and letting it rot or by burning it. It reminds me of a garbage can. Where is it coming from? Surely this can't possibly last longer than a few moments. It does.

The smell of a small bush fire follows the rancid. After that, the smell of salt and the sea reminds me of home and confirms my suspicion of where we are.

At the next stop, the old sleeping woman next to me gets off. Somehow she knew where we were. Perhaps it was the smell of the sea. A young woman fills her place. She looks my age although I'm not sure; it's hard to tell. She wears a *kanga*[5] tightly wrapped around her curvaceous body. She's slim, but not starving slim. She looks very healthy. She's been moulded

---

[5]   Printed cotton, rectangular fabric worn as a wrap-around skirt.

by beautiful genes and by a lifetime of never ending work and deprivation of luxuries. As she lifts the isle seat and turns to sit, I find her face with my wandering and adventurous eyes and she has already found mine. I smile and she returns before completing the complicated maneuver.

She is really beautiful. The *kanga* attempts to hide her beautiful body from me, but it does nothing. My imagination is as vivid on this shape as on any other. Her breasts are small but formed and demand attention. They are humble. The type I've grown to love since the days of the monstrous breasts of my testosterone driven youth. Her hair is short. Her hair is shaved. I love it and I don't know why. These women with shaved heads drive me absolutely crazy. They seem to be the most beautiful women in the world as if they were all chosen for their beauty and told they must keep their hair short for this is the way of the beautiful women. This is the way of the women who drive men mad. Her brilliant smile brings out mine as we exchange obliged greetings. The smile drives me crazy. A genuine, full felt smile, backed by assured happiness. No way is this smile fake. No way. I'm absolutely crazy over this smile and this hair.

At the next stop, the conductor yells some obscenity in Kiswahili. He wasn't paying attention as we rolled to a stop and he didn't see the police officer waiting amongst the crowd. I fail to see the apparently obvious problem with the police officer. Everyone else sees it and smacks their lips in disapproval. This smacking of the lips throws me off every time. I expect someone to chastise the smacker, but it does not come. This is not the way of the Darinians.

The officer steps out in front of the van and holds out his hand in an authoritative stopping motion. He is a policeman with a badge. He goes through the motions. He points to the blinkers, lights, and windshields one-by-one and the driver flips the appropriate switches to show that everything is in order. Both the conductor and driver continue to babble in annoyance.

For *daladala* professionals, time is money and this officer has severely cut into these gentlemen's time. Yet even I begin to suspect that time will not be the only commodity lost in this happenstance. The officer has something other than civil service on his agenda.

The officer walks over to the driver's side window and begins to argue. The reason for the argument is not important, just the argument itself. The act of arguing is what's important. After so long, he reaches into the car and grabs the keys out of the ignition. The conductor and driver explode with objections. They're to no avail. Only one thing carries a voice powerful enough to end this ordeal.

After a few perilous moments of furious argument, the driver smacks his lips and reaches into his short pocket. Immediately after, he finds the officer's hand with his. The officer steps back smiling and waving as we drive away.

At the stop we picked up a woman who is now standing in front of me. I get up and offer her my seat. I am a gentleman, an American. *Le Fille* has no idea.

The woman refuses, but I insist and she takes my seat. As she sits and rests her weary legs I can tell she is relieved. She did not want to be standing. Her relief relieves me. I am happy for her.

Now my ass is in the face of the girl of my dreams. The girl with the *kanga* and the short hair and the smile who comes from the land of beautiful women. I am wearing jeans and I wonder if Kanga thinks the same of my ass as I do of hers. Do women like men's asses? I've heard women suggesting they do, but it never seemed serious. They always seemed to be joking. I think though, that this is how women deceive men. They lead us to believe that they're not serious about things we hold dearly. Things like asses. They joke and laugh as if it's no big deal. I think it is a big deal. Very big.

From up here, standing in the *daladala*, I have a bird's eye view of the passengers. I don't think any of these people were on the bus when I got on. I am no longer the cute *mzungu*. The woman in front of me is writing a text message. Most of it is in Kiswahili, but in the middle, it reads, "haha, just joking. Yea right!" I wonder if she was talking about a man's ass and saw me looking.

The woman next to her is sitting patiently with her hands in her lap, looking straight ahead. She is holding a silk handkerchief and twirling one of its corners in her thumbs. It looks fun. I realise I've never owned anything silk. It seems to be a very pretty cloth, but what good is it. Can it absorb moisture? If it can, I doubt it's anything like cotton. Cotton is amazing. Now there's a great cloth, cotton.

I move on. The man in the window seat seems to be watching the road. Is he watching the dance of the road? I wonder who he likes in the dance, the road or the grass or the dirt. Maybe I should ask. He seems like a sophisticated man. He seems like he would like the cool and collective dance of the road with the yellow pinstripe. He's definitely a pinstripe man. That pinstripe defines him.

I watch the dance for a few moments and try to decipher its clues. Where are we? I can't tell. I've almost given up when I see that the curb has begun to dance. The curb is a downtown cat, a connoisseur of sorts. The curb does not dawdle in the affairs of the suburbs. We are close now, perhaps on the bridge. Ahh, yes, the sea's scent is stronger.

Suddenly we stop. I continue to move although the car has stopped. My body reacts to the surprise. I tighten the grip on the pole that's been welded to the side of the van. Thank you for putting that pole there, seriously. I try to reduce my intrusion onto other people, but there's no way to stop my body from lunging forward. I grab the man's shoulder in front of me with my other hand. He doesn't seem to mind. This isn't his first time in the sardine tin.

The car begins to move again and I feel the cold warmth of a hand behind me. Kanga has grabbed my waist to stop herself from lunging forward. I didn't feel it at first, but now, as she slowly loosens, I know that her grip was firm. She continues very slowly to loosen her grip. It's endless. Time has stood still. Finally, just as her hand has loosened, my full sensation returns and I feel her other hand slowly slipping off the pocket of my ass. Ha! Caught in the act. Kanga, you have ruined it for your sisters. Now I know for sure, women do love men's asses.

I ponder the thought. This has really opened up a whole new door in the world of men and women. Women can no longer passively ignore us. They must admit their defeat. But how will I tell the rest of the world? Nobody's going to believe me; this is ridiculous. Damn! Blasted women! One day you'll slip.

At the next stop, to my utter disappointment, Kanga slips past me to get off. As her face passes mine, I ponder the parting words to the woman who almost gave up the world's biggest secret to me. I can't think of anything. Perhaps the best response is silence. I want to get off with her, walk with her, pick flowers for her. No way, she's not worth it.

She gets off and turns back to the bus as we drive away. I look down at the window and meet her eyes. We are soaring. I know I need to get off, but I can't. I can't make any logical decisions. She waves goodbye from the side of the road. It's the sweetest wave in the world. Oh, Kanga!

The rest of the ride is a blissful existence while I drift in the world of my new love. *Le Fille* is over and done with. Kanga is in. I've been on this bus for forty five minutes, yet it feels like an eternity. I will stay on this bus forever.

I'm wakened from my daydream by the conductor.

"*Mzungu! Mzungu, vipi!*" he yells. I struggle to make sense of it. He continues, "*Shusha Mzungu. Hapa.*"[6]

---

[6]   Drop.

Finally, I snap out of it and gain my senses. I look around me. The bus is empty. The driver is looking back at me with a shit-eatin' grin. The conductor is still looking at me. People outside are beginning to notice. They are stopping to look into the *daladala* with the crazy *mzungu*. I gather my senses and step out. Wait, did I leave anything…no. I step out into the day and look around. It's bright and I have to squint my eyes to see. I begin to walk and the conductor grabs me.

"*Mzungu*," he says, "*mia mbili.*"

What? Oh, I haven't paid yet. I reach into my right pocket for the money. Not there. The left pocket. Nope. I look back into the *daladala*, on the floor. Nothing. The conductor is beginning to get aggravated. Desperately, I search my back pockets. I never put money in my back pockets. Yes! There's something there, its paper. It must be my bills. I pull the paper out and read it.

"*Tako zuri!*" nice ass.

"The Concealed Project"

by Zuhura Badru

It was a blue Monday morning. Mr. Mduma Kajanja was in his office enjoying the breeze, as his office was near the sea. He was still tired due to a weekend of drinking and late sleeping. He seemed to be thinking of something very important and maybe urgent. Suddenly, he grabbed the phone and called someone.

"Hello, ooh yes, it's me, Kajanja," he said, and proceeded, "Will you please come over? … Ooh, yes, now. It is urgent that you come at once." He listened for a while, then finished, "Ok. Later then." He put the receiver back and started to read some files.

His company dealt with clearing and forwarding, but he dealt with secret special services as well. This Monday, he had received some information that could bring him a lot of money with regard to one of the secret special services. For this reason, he had called his accomplice, Mr. Ishaji Fundi. Mr. Fundi was not different from Mr. Kajanja himself. As the saying goes, "Birds of a feather flock together."

In half an hour the two friends were sitting together in Mr. Kajanja's office. "Here I am, please tell me everything," said Mr. Fundi.

"It is good you have come. I received some information that could remove us from this life smelling of poverty," Kanja said.

Mr. Fundi, who had been listening without even blinking, said, "Tell me what we have to do for there is a smell of cash in your talk!"

Kajanja interrupted, "Now listen my friend, one of my friends from the Ministry of Community Development has just called."

"Go on, go on and please get to the point," said Fundi. He seemed to be in a hurry.

19

"Ok, ok. He told me that the government of the United States of Mbali has given funds for developing villages here in Sokomoko through their Embassy," he said and then took a deep breath as if he had been running.

"Do you mean Mbali, that very rich country? Then how do we come in?" asked Fundi.

"Don't be a fool, Fundi. We will get that cash either by hook or by crook, and those development projects in villages will be done theoretically, if you know what I mean." clarified Kajanja.

"Now I get it. I will call Alice to prepare the proposal so we can get that cash. She is good at cooking data, you know," Fundi said in satisfaction.

"I see you are using your brains. Don't forget: After we have the money, we will give some to that friend I mentioned, and of course some to village leaders and the business will be over," he said with a smile.

With this plan between these two old friends, the meeting was over. Each was thinking of the very big amount of money they were about to mine and use at the expense of other people's lives.

Two weeks later, they presented a proposal in which they had shown how three villages – Kisomo, Kasongo and Maendeleo – badly needed schools and a safe water supply system. They also presented some reports of previous projects done by their Non Governmental Organization that goes by the name Community Social Services Giving Organization (CSSGO). Kajanja's office was their main office and Miss Alice was the secretary. They were as busy as ants during those two weeks.

With Mr. Twalibu's connection in the Ministry, the CSSGO was given ten million dollars to build two good schools and to construct a water supply system in each village in one year.

Mr. Twalibu, from the Ministry of Communication Development, who happened to be Mr. Kajanja's friend, was appointed chairperson of the team designated to evaluate the project upon completion. The Committee that appointed him had no knowledge that he was Kajanja's friend. What a coincidence!

Another meeting took place in Kajanja's office: the three of them were celebrating the end of their poverty and the beginning of their path to prosperity. Bottles of whisky and wine were all over the place and drinking was the order of the time.

"Hey, now we have all that we need, let us draw up the plan for the distribution," said Kajanja.

"I think four million dollars will be enough to put up examples of schools and water systems in those villages," proposed Fundi.

"And what about the people's participation? The evaluation team will cause problems for sure," said Alice looking a bit worried.

"You should not worry, who cares about villagers' participation business? What we have to do is corroborate with village leaders and that will be enough," said Fundi with assurance.

"We have the advantage. As you all know, Twalibu is a good friend of mine, a little portion of cash will settle everything," added Kajanja.

"That, I had forgotten. So now we should set to work. You know it's not easy to corroborate with people nowadays; they are afraid of the government's long arm," said Miss Alice.

"That is the only difficult part – getting village leaders on our side. When we finish with them, we will be as free as air," said Kajanja.

Miss Alice added. "Oh, yes, as free as air," raising her hands in the air.

The project team from CSSGO set to work in the three villages. In Kasongo village, a Mr. Mkude sat in his office at a single table with a telephone and some files on it. The office had two chairs and the president's picture was on the wall. Mr. Mkude was waiting for someone who had called for an appointment. He was reading some files when a man appeared at the door.

"*Karibu*. I hope it's Mr. Kajanja," he said, while shaking the visitor's hand.

"Oh, thank you. You are right. I am Kajanja from the CSSGO," he said, smiling.

"You are welcome. Have a seat please," he said, pointing at the chair in front of the table.

"Thank you. I will not take much of your time. I am here to talk to you about the issue I mentioned on the phone a while ago," he said.

"Yes, you said something about the project and the report I should write, but will you explain please," he said.

"No problem. I am here to offer you a deal. We are supposed to build a good school and construct a water distribution system..."

Before he could finish, Mr. Mkude said, "That's very good, our village really needs those services. How do I help you?"

"We will do our job and you have a simple task, to write a report in our favour. I promise you, you will not regret this. It's a chance that happens once in a life time," Kajanja said.

"To be honest, you are confusing me. Will you please explain?" Mkude requested.

"I mean that your report should not consider what we will do or the quality of services we will provide. You should write a report that our services are of high quality. We will pay you handsomely," he assured Mkude.

"Now I understand, but things are not so simple; the government might be watching." He paused for a while and then continued, "What about the evaluation team and the village committee?" He sounded very worried.

"About the evaluation team we have no problem at all, that is settled. Concerning the village committee, you should settle them. Don't forget, you are their leader," said Kajanja.

"That is ok, but it will cost you a fortune. You should remember that I am risking my job here," said Mkude.

"Don't worry. Now you should be saying goodbye to all your financial problems. Trust me my friend," said Kajanja.

"So, when do I get my money? I need this to be fast," he said.

"Not so fast, my friend. I will come with my colleagues for further negotiations and payments. You will write that report after we have completed the project," said Kajanja.

"Ok. You and your friends are welcome any time, and I promise you the report is not a problem. If you want, you can write it and let me copy it over," said Mkude.

"Oh, thank you. I will leave now," he said and stood up.

"You are welcome. I am at your service," said Mkude, waving goodbye.

Mr. Kajanja left satisfied. He was thinking of how the job had been more simple than he had expected. "I can't believe he did not give me much trouble. Oh such an ignorant fellow, he did not even consider the possibility that I might be a security officer. Now I believe money is the opium of the mind," Kajanja said to himself.

At the next village known as Maendeleo, the negotiation was done between Mr. Daudi and Mr. Fundi. The former had graduated from Sokomoko University three years before and was now working as an agricultural officer in Maendeleo village. He was elected village leader because the community wanted a leader who is educated, believing he will be of help in the development of their community.

It was a little difficult getting Mr. Daudi on their side, but after the promise of six thousand and four hundred dollars, the matter was settled.

The project team was successful in their plan in Kasongo and Maendeleo villages. Schools of low quality were built at the lowest cost; laboratories were not built; and a single toilet was built for the staff and students. Village leaders were given their portion of cash and fake reports were written in favour of the CSSGO.

Villagers were so happy to have services that they had been requesting for a long time. They did not know that what they were given was not even half of what they were supposed to get.

Things did not go smoothly for the CSSGO in Kisomo village. In this village, the plan stumbled on the block and the stumbling block was Miss Mariam, the village chairperson. She was a teacher at Kisomo High School. She had graduated from Sokomoko University in the same year with Mr. Daudi of Maendeleo village. Miss Mariam was known for her character as a principled person. As the vice president of the students' union at the university, she had exposed the president's misuse of the union's funds. No one had done such a thing before, as the president had power and influence. After that incident, Mariam was given the name "the Sun" because she had managed to expose the president's dark secrets. Some people say she was so upright due to her family's background as her father was a pastor.

One morning, she had a visitor in her office, non other than Mr. Fundi from the CSSGO. When he mentioned the whole plan, she did not panic. She stayed calm and told him, "If you want to do any dirty business, go ahead, but I will not cooperate." She paused and proceeded, "I want you to know that nothing and more specifically no amount of money will be enough to buy my dignity or convince me to do anything that I know is wrong."

Mr. Fundi realised the task was going to be difficult, so he tried to threaten her. "You know miss, you can easily lose your job, and your principles will not help you. Don't you know that money can do anything?" Fundi hoped his new strategy would work.

"I am ready for anything. You should know I do what's right, not what's easy or convenient," she answered, before sending him out of her office. Fundi was out of words so Mariam added "Mr. whatever your name is – provide the services you are supposed to or prepare to be behind bars. I will not write a fake report in your favour," she said and asked him to close the door behind him.

After that incident Miss Mariam planned to have a word with Mr. Daudi of Maendeleo village, so she could get some advice. The next day she went to Maendeleo; it was only a two hour ride by bus. She was surprised with Mr. Daudi's perception of the matter. He acted as if writing a fake report, misusing the fund, and jeopardizing people's lives was as simple as killing a mosquito.

"Lord, what has come over you, Daudi, how can you be so cynical?" she asked, almost in tears.

"Poor you, do you still think being patriotic while dying poor is being brave?" he asked seriously.

"You used to be principled. What happened after we graduated? Do you mean Sokomoko University did not teach you any values or manners?" asked Miss Mariam.

"It truly did, but what we think of the world while at the University is different from what we find in real life. This country has a lot of inadequate policies. If they change and promote a good life for me and others, I swear I will stick to my principles," he said.

"Principles are principles, right is right, and what is wrong is wrong. You cannot blame hard ships or policies on something you can do right," she said.

It seemed Daudi was tired of the argument, so he said "We don't have to argue anymore. You either take it or leave it. By the way, what is a paper and words written on it in exchange for enough cash to start a good business?"

"It is not about faking a report. It is about people's lives, about integrity and the development of the whole of Sokomoko," she said.

"Ok, Miss Good Manners, you can now leave. It seems neither of us is giving in," suggested Daudi.

"I will leave Daudi, but I am warning you. You either change now or wait for the gathering cyclone to swallow you," she said while leaving.

At the end of the project, Miss Mariam wrote the appropriate report concerning that project. She also decided to go to town to talk to the person responsible for the evaluation of the project done by the CSSGO. Mr Twalibu told her that the Ministry was so grateful and more specifically that he himself was very grateful. He told her that the information she gave would be a secret for her safety and that justice would be done. Miss Mariam left with joy that she had done a good job as a responsible Sokomoko citizen.

Miss Mariam was waiting for some disciplinary steps to be taken, but she waited in vain. She kept hoping Mr. Twalibu would contact her concerning the matter, but it seemed he had disappeared like a ghost or a spirit. Months passed by and there was no news: only that Mr. Daudi had bought two big farms and one car. On the other hand, Mr. Mkude of Kasongo village married two young women at the same time in addition to the one he had already, and built a new house. To him, this was heavenly prosperity.

Miss Mariam could no longer wait. She decided to go to town again and see Mr. Twalibu. She was depressed when he told her that the project done by the CSSGO was a shining success and nothing was seriously wrong. Miss Mariam could not believe her ears; she had to shake her head to make sure she was not dreaming. She went home heart broken. She knew that she had to do something, but could not figure it out. She sat down very tired and thought, "No wonder this country has gone nowhere in spite of the fact that it has enjoyed independence for over a solid forty five years."

"Corruption has been going on in this country for quite a long time and it has to be put to an end," she said to herself. She planned to go to Mbali's Embassy and talk to those who had funded the project so they would know that the CSSGO had a concealed project behind the genuine development project.

For a week she tried to talk to someone at the Embassy, but it was fruitless. When she was about to give up for the first time in her life, she was lucky to meet Mr. Gordon Boric, the general secretary of the social services department at the Embassy. She spent more than an hour explaining how she had tried to deal with the problem in different ways, but failed.

In two months, the Embassy's investigation was done. As a result, the government was forced to investigate as well and Mr. Daudi and Mr. Mkude were imprisoned for three years each. Mr. Twalibu was expelled from his job, his belongings were confiscated, and he was imprisoned for five years. Kajanja and his fellows were caught at the airport trying to escape. They were imprisoned for seven years each and all their assets were confiscated to compensate for the misused fund.

When Mariam went to prison to see Daudi about a month later, he could not look at her face. He was ashamed of himself. Mariam told him, "Don't look back, just change for now and the future," and then she went away.

That was not all. Mariam was appointed to take over Mr. Twalibu's position at the Ministry. The government came to realise that she could manage the position without difficulties, besides, she had done several courses on community development. The post was to be challenging enough, howeer, with her determination, she managed and helped several other staff member under her to change for the better.

"The Total Crisis"

by Simon Mlundi

It was a cool sunny day. The sun was smiling gently, rising from the east majestically. The wind kept blowing as smoothly and slowly as a chameleon's motion, denoting existence. It was a Friday evening in September 2005 at Kiberiti Secondary School in Mililani District in the Coastal region.

I will never forget this day.

Life was very difficult, as hard as a sedimentary rock. On this day, I lost all my best friends; I lost all my fellow students; I lost my teachers; I lost all my relatives. My best friends turned to be my greatest enemies. I was like a dying cockroach lying with its legs up in the air. I was like a lost sheep, far from the pasture.

All my relatives considered me a fool like a burning candle eating its own body to benefit people's vision. No body listened to me; no body believed me; no body understood me; no body talked to me. To them I was a liar, a great liar. This event I named "The Total Crisis."

Several years back, when I was young, we were a happy family. My mother was a doctor at Muhimbili National Hospital. Things started falling apart when my mother became paralysed. She was very sick. We were taken to the country side to a village called Shelui in Singida region to our grandmother's home. In my entire life I never saw my father because the one who was to show me my father is now paralysed, unable even to talk. So I grew up without knowing my father.

I, my elder brother Noel, and my second brother Nelson started to live in the rural area. We grew crops, kept domestic animals such as sheep, goats, and cattle, and took good care of both our mother and grandmother.

Generally, my life was very miserable. I studied at Shelui Primary School. Noel was taken to our aunt who lives in

Mbeya. Nelson died in 2000. Despite every thing, I passed my primary examination and I was selected to join form one in 2000 at Shelui Secondary School in Singida.

Life was still very difficult. From primary school to secondary, I used *kibatari* for studying. That small kerosene lamp produced smoke like a train. I had no support from any side. I had no money for school fees, no money for tuition, and no money for school items such as books, uniforms, and the other necessaries for a student.

I lost the sky and I lost the ground when my mother travelled the journey of no return on the 12th March 2002. We were very sad and our eyes shed tears like ocean water. We lost an important pole in our family, the only hope we had. Life became even more complicated.

One day, my grandmother told me an important thing which acts as my weapon. She said, "Simyoon, you are now an orphan; you are a parentless child. Life is a journey, a very long journey. You will climb mountains, walk valleys of death, sail rivers and oceans fighting against big tides and waves. The only parent you have is a book. Pray and study hard."

I realised that I had one special Supreme Being who always takes good care of me. That is God. He never abandons his servants. I prayed hard while studying. I completed form four in 2003. I passed and was selected to join form five at Kiberiti High School in Mililani.

Personally, I was very happy and I thanked the Almighty God millions of times for giving me this very special chance. I asked myself, who am I to be given this chance? How many students wanted this opportunity? Am I more righteous compared to them? The answer was no, the big NO. It was only God's mercy.

While I was still celebrating my victory, my cousin Theophilus told me, "It's true that you celebrate now, but how will you go to school?" I replied, "I don't understand, what do you mean?"

He said, "I mean where are you going to get your school fees?" That is when my celebration turned to sadness. I had no body to support me. All my relatives told me that there would be no school fees; therefore, instead of me going to school, I should look for a job like being a primary school teacher or a policeman.

Personally, I hated this idea. Therefore I strongly opposed this proposal. I wanted to fulfil my dreams of continuing with my advanced lessons so as to go to the university. This opposition annoyed them very much.

My aunt who lives in Dar es Salaam invited me to go visit her. In spite of being poor, she is very kind and generous. Women like her should be rich so as to help the poor. This was my first day to travel from the rural area to a city by bus.

We started to look for someone to assist me with school fees. Finally the Kinondoni Municipal Council agreed to support me by paying my school fees as I was an orphan. So I went to Kiberiti High School and, in fact, my lessons went on well.

One day, students demonstrated in order to force the government to provide services such as electricity, water, medicine, and some means of transport which seemed to have been forgotten. It was during the general election campaign. Students addressed the Honourable Kitambi, who was contesting the presidential position through the ruling party, to express their problems. The demonstration was accompanied by rioting and the destruction of such properties as the headmaster's house.

Knowing myself and my life, knowing my family and our economic status, knowing the consequences of demonstration, I decided not to participate in the riot. The Regional Commissioner, Honourable Dangani, came to resolve the problem and, in fact, he resolved it.

After completing mock examinations in September 2005, we closed the school for the last holiday. Every student was very happy to have this holiday after being at school for a long time.

I went to spend my holiday in Dar es Salaam where I attended tutorial classes at Chang'ombe.

Then came the day, the day that I will always regret for my whole life.

When I was on my way to Chang'ombe, I met my best friend Judah. Judah asked me, "Have you found another school, Simon?"

"Another school! Why? What for?" I asked. "Don't you have the news?" he asked me.

"News! What news?"

"Simon, I have bad news for you!"

I interrupted, "Bad news!"

"Yes, bad news. I'm sorry to inform you that you have been dismissed from school!"

"Dismissed from school! Why?"

"Demonstration, remember! You led the demonstration. They said that you were the king, the ring leader of all the problems that occurred at Kiberiti."

"Judah, you are the only friend I have. I know that you know me better than any body. Do you think I'm capable of committing a crime like that? Tell me where did I do wrong?"

"Simon, I know you better. I know what you are capable of and what you are not capable," said Judah.

"Why do they do this to me?"

"If there is something that affected how people see you, it must be your sweet tongue; I mean you have the power to persuade."

"I'm doomed!" I said.

"By the way," said Judah, "Don't worry about Irene. She is in good hands; she will be under my control."

"Is this the right moment to talk about women?" I asked, adding, "You only think of women."

"You always try to approach the girl of my life. Now Irene is mine, mine alone. Before I forget, I will also be the first winner in our class in academic matters. No obstacles any more. I win; you lose; that is life!"

"I can't believe my ears." I said.

"Some times, you should expect the unexpected," was all that Judah said.

Though I was the tallest boy in our school, I realised at that moment that I was as small as an ant. I lost energy and fell down. I felt my small head was carrying the whole world. My eyes became as red as glowing fire and full of blood tears. This was not only the end of the world, but also the end of all my dreams.

The next day I decided to go to school to confirm whether it was true that I had been dismissed. The headmaster verified that it was true. I asked permission to take all my belongings to my home as there was no school any more. Before even several seconds, the headmaster, Simba Mkali, came with five policemen to arrest me. They accused me of organizing the riot. I was as angry as an injured lion.

I was taken to the police station. I reacted very strongly as I did not want to be jailed. Finally I realised I was just a grasshopper trying to fight an elephant. "May you please listen to me, police officer? You are trying to arrest an innocent boy," I said.

That police man shouted, "Innocent boy! Are you innocent?"

"Yes, I am; I didn't lead the demonstration. I didn't participate in the riot. During the demonstration, I went to sleep in the street."

"How can we believe you when your fellows named you, you, as the leader."

"You can ask any body, even my friend," I said.

"Who is your friend?" he asked.

"My best friend is called Judah John. He knows me better and he is the only one who can verify that I am innocent."

"Who did you say is your witness?"

"He is Judah John." He opened the big file which was on the old table and took out a letter.

"Judah has already witnessed. Have a look at this letter." I was relieved and, smiling, took that letter. This is what my friend wrote:

NAME of the LEADER of the DEMONSTRATION

Please refer to the above mentioned subject. My name is Judah John. I'm a student at this school and I'm in Form Six this year. I would like to mention the name of the person who led the last demonstration that took place at our school as well as to explain how the demonstration went on step by step, as I was asked. The name of the person who led the demonstration is Simon Amos. He is a very bad seed in our school.

I was there during the demonstration and I witnessed every incident taking place. The first day, he told me that the Honorable Kitambi is coming to our region for the campaign of the coming general election. He also told of his ambition of uniting all students to demonstrate in order to force the government to provide services such as medicine, a school bus, electricity, the renovation of old buildings, as well as food.

The same night Simon's people came to every dormitory and woke up us all to go to the meeting. Being my best friend, I spent most of my time advising him not to do something like that because doing so would jeopardise his life. He covered his ears with cotton. He called me a woman and a coward. Simon has a sweet tongue that made every student accept to cooperate with him. I wanted to tell the school administration of what was going on, but they threatened that if a student speaks out, blood would be their right; that they would kill him or her. So I became a watch man; a silent one.

One night before the day of the demonstration, Simon organised all students to demonstrate the next day. That folllowing day, students woke up early and went to the demonstration. We slept on the main road to await the presidential contestant, Ndugu Kitambi.

When the Honourable Kitambi arrived, he found students sleeping on the road. With courage like a lion, Simon stood up majestically and expressed to Kitambi all the problems facing this school and how they hinder student performance. The Regional Commissioner promised to comeand resolve the problem.

The RC failed to come, so Simon organised a riot to destroy school property. This riot was stopped by police. Simon ran to hide on the street. That's how the demonstration and the riot went on and that is how Simon Amos led the destruction of our school. Other students who participated in the demonstration are form five, whose names I do not know. For the good of our school, bad seeds should be uprooted.

Thank you very much.

Yours faithfully,

Judah John (student)

After reading this letter, I lost all energy and I collapsed. I didn't believe that the one whom I considered to be my best friend could spit in my face like this; the one I considered my blood brother who would protect and be on my side would turn to be the fire burning my life like this. I didn't know the reasons for spiting on me in this way. The police carried me and threw me into the cell where I fell on the floor like a bag of maize.

They locked me in ready to be taken to court on the following Wednesday. That would make a total of five days given the fact that it was only Friday.

In the cell I was welcomed by beautiful songs sung by mosquitoes. This jail was very small with an even smaller window. I was boxed in this small room. You cannot differentiate day and night in such a cell. Bedbugs and ticks were very happy and started to prepare for supper after starving for several weeks.

The smell of decayed animal combining with a mixture of urine and excrement made the room well perfumed. And, in fact, I was well perfumed by that rotten smell. I had to stand up throughout the night because I could not sit down where there is urine, excrement, and bad bugs with other small insects which bit me hard as if they were taking revenge for staying without food for a long time. Throughout the night I couldn't sleep. I moved to and fro. I sat; I stood or even sometimes looked outside through the small hole. I admired how the moon was shining happily and freely.

In the beginning, I tried to chase the mosquitoes which celebrated my blood. After being tired, I left them to suck the blood of this innocent boy. The mosquitoes feasted throughout the night: millions of them drank millions of litres.

My anger grew as does fire in dry bush, not because of being terminated from school, but because of being chased and locked in jail for a crime I did not commit.

In the distance, I heard the Headmaster's voice. At the beginning, I thought that he had come to release me. Contrary to my expectations, I heard him telling the police officer: "Take this envelope."

"What is that huge amount of money for?" the policeman asked him!

"Sssshiii! Make sure that that boy rots in jail for many years."

"But why sir?"

"You know I hate him because he destroyed my expensive properties."

"Anyway, you can count on me," said the officer.

"Thank you," said the Headmaster while leaving.

I realised that for me to be set free would be like trying to capture air. I remembered the true friend who never abandoned me. I prayed throughout that night. "Oh my God! The God who unlocked Paul and Syrah, remember you said that you are the father of orphans and husband of widows; again, you said that you will never abandon me in the valley of death. Please Father, perform a miracle for me this day. If I am guilty, let me rot in jail, but, if I am really innocent, set me free tomorrow."

I kept on praying and crying. For the first time, I spoke an unknown language. I heard a voice calling me, saying "Simon, Simon, I will never leave you!"

It was a cool morning, which I realised by the cock crowing, because it was still dark. I heard the door of the cell opening. The police officer told me, "Take your waste out to the latrines." I carried the bucket outside and poured the contents in the toilet.

The long night of suffering and that voice I heard in the night gave me courage to speak to that policeman on the morning shift. I told him, "Please police officer, I know you are a human being and you know that not all people in jail have committed crimes. I'm not justifying myself, whether I'm innocent or not. But I only ask you to please set me free. Problems are present for all people. Today I have a problem; tomorrow it can be for any body. Please give me a chance so as to rebuild my life."

That policeman looked at my swollen eyes, red like a ripe tomato. His eyes started to drop tears as well. He said, "I will set you free and if your headmaster comes, I will tell him that your parents came to release you. And when you go there, do anything possible to get an education." So the police officer advised me as he set me free.

To me it was a mere daydream. God answered my prayer and it was a miracle. I thanked that police officer and I went to Dar es Salaam. I met with my fellow students who were terminated and we appealed to the regional headquarters which is in Kibaha. Here also I found one copy of Judah's testimony against me. I was very angry and I thought of revenging myself on him, but I remembered a scripture saying, "Love your enemies...." I was happy to see two students who mentioned the real leaders of the demonstration. One of these was Irene, who wrote a true testimony about me.

At home, with the exception of my aunt Suzy, who kept on crying and praying to the Almighty God, my relatives isolated me. I had no body to speak to; I had no friends. No neighbours. No body believed me. No body listened to me. Although I was free, life became more miserable. I stayed there for one month.

In October 2005, my aunt who lives in Mbeya came and told me that she had found a school for me in Mbeya. I was very impressed by this news. I went with her to the Mbeya Sai area. Contrary to my expectations, my aunt made me into a donkey, a little houseboy. There was no school any more. I did all the domestic work such as mopping the floor, washing clothes including underwear, cooking, feeding domestic animals such as pigs, dogs, cattle, and chickens. Fetching water and farming activities became my daily responsibilities. I woke up at 5am and slept at 11pm every day. I stayed there for four months. I had no time even for touching a book.

On December 20th 2005, I received a letter from the Regional Education Officer informing me that our appeal was accepted so we were allowed to go back to school. We were to report on the 31st of December. When we arrived there, the school administrators were reluctant to welcome us as they had appealed the decision to the Ministry of Education. So they refused to receive us.

We had to go back to Kibaha and this time the Regional Commissioner wrote a letter ordering the school to receive us. They also refused until the general secretary of the Ministry of Education called them. They allowed us to rejoin the school on condition that we pay all outstanding fees, write a declaration letter, and come with our parents. I had not even a single cent. I went to town but nobody had money. Finally, my brother Noel gave me 20,000 Tsh which enabled me to go back to school.

So ten days before the national examinations we were allowed to rejoin the school. While students were celebrating graduation day on Saturday, I was arriving. I had only ten days to study and on Monday we started to do the exams.

Throughout these nine days I had two jobs: Studying hard and praying hard. We finally completed our examinations peacefully. I was very happy to be one of the form six leavers.

I went to Dar es Salaam. When the results were out, I could not believe my eyes: I had performed wonderfully. All my enemies shut their mouths. To show that God never fails, I was selected to join the University of Dar es Salaam that same year. My studies went on well at the University.

One day I met my best friend Irene on the main campus. I asked her, "Where are you, my dear Irene?"

"I'm at the Institute of Social Work taking a degree in Human Resource Management. I was very happy when I saw your results. Congratulations!"

"Thanks! By the way, where is your fiancé Judah?"

"Firstly, that red Satan is not my fiancé, and secondly, he failed the exams and so he is drinking *mbege* and *chang'aa* in the country side. Furthermore, the rumour is that he is married to two wives."

"That's life." I said sadly.

Testimony

by Emmanuel Lema

Sundown

It was getting dark and she had walked for two hours. What worried her was that she had not seen a house or even a hut on her way from the bus stop. She continued walking, but she could not stop wondering what was wrong with the vast land she crossed. It could not get into her head that such a vast land could remain uninhabited or uncultivated.

Slowly darkness was starting to fall and she had not seen any sign of peoples' settlement. "How far is it still to the village?" she asked herself while walking up a hill. She seemed to be tired, thirsty, and hungry, but she kept on walking along a corrugated narrow road. As she came on top of a hill, she smiled.

From the hill, she could see faint lights and smoke in the valley. "That must be a village," she shouted as if she had seen something scary. She started to run down the hill, while her hands supported the small bag on her head…

Darkness had already fallen on the land and all villagers were indoors. Women and their elder daughters were busy preparing supper, while boys were sitting with their fathers in their compounds.

However, Rumishaeli was still in the bush near the village. He had gone to check if there was a rabbit caught in a trap he had put there. He was good at trapping rabbits and only on a few occasions had he missed a rabbit for supper. He came out of the bush holding a rabbit in one hand and his trap and *panga*[7] in the other. He walked very fast toward the village. It was very dark and quiet. He did not expect to meet anyone at that time in that darkness, but, to his surprise, he saw someone running down a hill that was not very far from where he was standing.

---

[7] Machete

"Who could that be?" he asked himself amid surprise and fear. He wanted to run, but his legs started to betray him. Footsteps could now be heard not far from where he was standing.

He thought quickly of what to do and concluded that he had better wait and see who it was. He hoped that it was a villager who had gone on a trip and was coming home late. Nevertheless, his question remained, "Who could that person be?"

He stood still on the roadside giving way to that unknown person. Suddenly there appeared before him a girl carrying a small bag on her head. She had not seen Rumishaeli and was about to pass him when he called out, "Hi, who are you?" The girl abruptly stopped and turned around. She threw her bag and started to run, but it was too late for her for Rumishaeli had gotten hold of her hand. "Don't run, don't run! Look here I am not a bad person, I won't hurt you!" said Rumishaeli. He had control of the girl's hand so she could not run away.

She was shaking with fear. "Please don't harm me. I am begging you please," she said, and burst into tears.

"Don't worry, I won't hurt you. I am here to help you," Rumishaeli assured her. "You see, am carrying a rabbit, a trap, and a *panga*. I am coming from the bush where I collected this," Rumishaeli told her, while pointing at the rabbit.

The girl was now assured of her safety. She looked at Rumishaeli in his face and they smiled at each other. "Do you live in this village?" Rumishaeli asked her.

"No, I don't. I'm… I mean I, I have never been here before," she struggled to make herself understood. Rumishaeli looked puzzled by her answer. The girl understood that her answers had created confusion for the boy standing before her. She also knew that there in the middle of nowhere, she only had this boy to help her get to her destination, the destination she had longed for, all the nights and days of the past two months. She coughed and talked.

"I am coming from Donga where I was born and raised and my final destination is Ruga village where my grandparents and mother once lived. My grandfather was called Kundaeli and my grandmother was called Bilha. I unfortunately never saw them but, my late mother told me about them, about this village, and about my brother."

Rumishaeli was surprised. "Please tell me your name and your mother's too," he said.

"My name is Sholanda and my mother's is Nsia."

"You said your mother's name is Nsia?" asked Rumishaeli.

Sholanda looked straight into his eyes, but she could not see much of him because of the darkness. "Please take me where my grandparents once lived," pleaded Sholanda.

"But your grandparents are no longer alive," Rumishaeli responded with a trembling voice. His hands let go of the rabbit, trap, and *panga*. He started sweating.

"I know that, but I was told by my mother that I will find my brother there…" She stopped talking after she realised that the boy was crying. "Ooh no, no, no. Please forgive me if I have offended you in anyway please," Sholanda looked confused.

"So you are Nsia's daughter?" Rumishaeli found strength to ask at last.

Rumishaeli threw himself to Sholanda and hugged her; he could not control himself from crying. "My…my…my name is Rumishaeli and I was told my mother was called Nsia, daughter of Kundaeli and Bilha," he talked amid sobs…

Nsia's heart started to beat very fast. While still in the hands of Rumishaeli, she remembered her mother's last words: "*I want you to go to the village and never come back to the city, my dear. When you meet your brother, tell him I am sorry, ask him to forgive his mother because she could not take care of him, she ran away from him because she ceased to exist the day she was raped. Also, tell him about my illness and my death…*"

Nsia was the last-born and the only daughter in *Mzee*[8] Kundaeli and his wife Bilha's family of six children. She was born and raised in Ruga village. She was loved by everyone in their village.

Men and boys admired her because of her beauty and hardworking character. When she was still very young, her aunt once told her mother, "My sister you are blessed with a beautiful little girl. When she grows, she will carry our village name to all four ends of the world."

Bilha did not believe her sister's words until Nsia turned four years old; then she started to see how beautiful her daughter was becoming each day. Men and boys could not stop talking about Nsia whenever they saw her. Boys would talk about her in school, on the way home from school. Men would talk about her as they drank local beer, and women and girls would talk about her when they were fetching water or walking to and from market.

There is a story that is still being told in Ruga: One evening a strange woman stood on top of a hill near the village and proclaimed that a girl would be born in Ruga and that she would be the queen of the land. It is still said that the strange woman went on to say, "…as the saying goes, 'an antelope in a jungle will fall on the lion's roar; this will befall the queen daughter of the land."

The story is told until today that this woman was an oracle's angel living in the forest and that she disappeared after delivering the oracle's message. For many years, the people of Ruga kept asking themselves if there was any truth in the woman's words. They waited to see if the woman's words would come true. As years passed, almost every villager had forgotten about the prophecy. However, one day, as six women were returning to the village from *shamba*,[9] they met Nsia on the way. They suddenly kept

---

[8] Title for an old person (it can also be used to address a respectable person regardless of his age).

[9] The fields.

silent. It was *Mama Bere* who broke the silence when she asked, "Isn't she as beautiful as the queen of our land?" Knowing she was not understood she added, "I mean the queen the strange woman prophesied longtime ago?"

"What are you talking about *Mama Bere?*" asked another woman, but they could not continue talking as Nsia had approached and greeted them. They responded to her greeting with smiles and, when she had passed, they could not but continue with the topic *Mama Bere* had started; they could not avoid speaking about Nsia's beauty. She was in every woman's mouth.

When Nsia was fourteen years old, her life changed tremendously. She lost both parents. The first one to die was her mother. It did not take long before her father followed. Her father's death was not shocking news in the village: Not because he was not a respected man, but because of the belief people had in the saying that if a wife dies first, the husband will follow shortly. Nsia was left with her five brothers.

Soon after the death of their father, four of Nsia's brothers left the village. They did not say where they were going, but it came to be known after three years. News about where they had gone did not come as good news to their brother and sister. Reports came to Ruga that four boys from that village who had been at Meremeta diamond mines were among many small scale miners who had died after they were buried alive in one of the mine holes following heavy rains. It was very easy to trace who those four boys were because only Nsia's brothers were missing in the entire village.

Nsia could not believe her brothers had died, leaving the two of them alone—just Nsia and Kiko, her youngest brother. Not so many months passed after the news about the four brothers' deaths before Nsia lost her only remaining family member. She woke up one day and found her brother missing from their hut. She looked for him everywhere, but she could not find him. At noon, shocking news came to the village that Kiko's body was found hanging from an *mruka*[10] tree on the border between Ruga and Mkombozi villages.

People found a written message on his body. It was through that message that people learned that Kiko had committed suicide because of what he called fear of failing to provide for himself and his sister. He wrote that it was better to die than to live poor. Ruga villagers were not surprised because they knew how lazy Kiko was. One old man was heard saying that, "*The Grave is a home for cowards and lazy people.*"

Nsia was left alone. She was her own father, mother, and brother; She had her life all to herself. This life became very difficult for her, but she kept fighting, believing in herself. One day, as she was going home from the river where villagers fetched water, Nsia met *Mama Bere*. They spent time talking about many things.

As Nsia was about to say goodbye, *Mama Bere* told Nsia, "My daughter, there is one thing I wanted to tell you." She continued, "Everyone in this village knows that you are the most beautiful girl in the village. You should find a man to marry you, my dear. There are a lot of good men out there." Nsia felt shy. She had never heard anyone talking to her about such things.

Mama Bere looked at her and knew Nsia was feeling uneasy. She continued, "My dear, remember you no longer have a family to look after you and life here in the village is as difficult as you see. Do not waste your beauty here, my daughter." She moved closer to Nsia, put her right hand on her left shoulder, and said, "I will see you tonight, my dear. Just go and think about what I have told you." She left and Nsia remained standing there puzzled for about three minutes. What she had just heard was strange to her. She had never thought of being married. "No, no, no it can't be. Not yet," she told herself as she resumed her walk back home. The bucket of water she was carrying on her head

---

[10]   An indigenous tree found in Kilimanjaro.

became heavier than it was before.

That night as Nsia was about to go to bed, she heard a knock on the door. "Who could that be at this time of the night?" she asked herself. "Nsia, Nsia it's me, my dear." She heard the voice she recognised to be *Mama Bere's*. She opened the door and *Mama Bere* entered the hut. "*Karibu Mama Bere*[11], have a seat and let me give you something to eat. You know I cooked *ng'andi*[12] today," Nsia told *Mama Bere,* but she did not want to eat anything. "Thank you, my dear, but I will not eat, you see I have to hurry back home. I have just brought someone with me, my dear. He will talk to you as I wait outside. Do not worry; everything will be alright my beautiful girl."

She finished talking, but she did not give Nsia time to say anything. She opened the door and waved at someone outside. A man entered the house. *Mama Bere* looked at Nsia who was in shock and whispered to her, "Talk to His Excellency, my daughter. He is going to give you the world you deserve. Do not let me down, ok!" She went outside.

Nsia came back to her senses. She could see everything clearly and understood it was not a dream but a real thing happening. A man was standing in front of her, in her own hut at night. She started to tremble as the man approached her and held her hand. "How are you Nsia?" She could not find strength to respond. She pulled her hand from his. It ached a little, but she was able to get herself free from his hand. "Do not feel frightened, dear," he coughed and continued. "I think you know me, Nsia, I am not a stranger to you. I am the son of this land. My parents were born and buried here. I was born here too, so I am not a stranger, Nsia."

Nsia could not hear everything he said; she had travelled miles away from there. She could not understand what had brought

---

[11] Welcome Bere's mother.

[12] Traditional Chagga food (mashed bananas and meat)

that politician to her hut. She knew the man standing before her. He was the most popular and wealthy person from their village in the entire country. He was a Member of Parliament for his Kisareni constituency and Minister for Finance in the government of the Republic of Danganyika for twelve years. His name was mentioned everywhere, His Excellency Tupa.

Nsia could not hold back her tears. Within a very short time, her cheeks were wet and tears kept running down as if there was ice melting in her eyes.

"Stop crying Nsia, stop. You don't have to." His Excellency Tupa drew himself closer to Nsia and put his hands around her waist. She struggled to get them off, but she could not.

"Let go of me, let go of me please…" she cried.

"You know, Nsia, you are the most beautiful girl in my entire constituency," His Excellency forced his words into Nsia, who was struggling to escape his hands. "I have travelled all the way from the city to come and take you. I want to marry you and give you a good life." It was not easy to get his hands off her body because he was holding her tightly.

"Let me go. I don't want to be married, I don't want I … *Mama Bere* please help," she cried aloud.

Ten minutes after Nsia had called out for help, *Mama Bere* could not hear Nsia crying anymore. She was not sure what was going on inside. She kept waiting outside in the dark and cold.

She started to lose patience and, as she was about to go to the door, the door opened from inside and His Excellency came out.

"What happened? Tell me is she ok?" she asked, but she did not wait for an answer. She went inside the hut. "Ooh my God, why did you rape her? Why?…" she cried.

"Nsia! Nsia!"

"*Abe mama!*"

"Please come... I have to go. I am late you know. *Osha hizi sahani hapa wateja wanakaribia kuja. Halafu bia zilizoko kwenye friji hazitoshi ongeza.*[13] I will be back before two."

"*Sawa, mama.*"[14]

"*Eeh, halafu atakuja Rama leo, usiniangushe. Changamkia tenda mrembo...*"[15] Nsia closed the door without saying anything more to that woman. She had about fifty plates to wash and beers to stack in the fridge before customers arrived.

One month after Nsia was raped by His Excellency Tupa, she noticed changes in her body. She was pregnant. She cried and cried everyday. She blamed and hated *Mama Bere* because it was because of her that she was raped. For days and months she did not go out as she used to. *Mama Bere* tried to console her, but she did not even want to see her.

Nine months passed and Nsia gave birth to a baby boy. She silently went to a woman called *Nkanambo* living in a nearby village and gave birth there. She had known the woman ever since her mother was alive. She twice came to their house and from conversations she used to have with Nsia's mothers, Nsia came to understand one day that she was a medicine woman. Nsia stayed with *Nkanambo* for two months.

One day she went back to her village, but she did that in the evening. As she stood near her hut, she thought for a while, then she decided she could no longer continue living in the village after what had happened. Whenever she remembered the night she was raped, she cried a lot. It was that night that she lost her virginity by force. "Now I have a baby, ooh, no, no, I must leave today and go somewhere, anywhere," she told herself. She had

---

[13] "Wash these plates, soon customers will soon be arriving. Beer in the fridge won't be enough, add more bottles."

[14] "All right mother."

[15] "Rama will come today, don't let me down. Grab the opportunity pretty girl."

kept some money in her hut. She had sold *ndizi mshare*[16] before she left. It was her only means to get to a place she believed she could hide herself away from Ruga villagers. She took the money and looked for a piece of paper and a pencil in the hut. She wrote something on that piece of paper and left the hut.

The following morning Nkanambo did not find Nsia in her room. Only her baby was lying in a bed made of a box. She wandered in the room and her wide eyes fell on a piece of paper near the baby. On it was written, "I am sorry mama. I had no choice but to leave. I cannot face my boy when he grows up and asks about his father. Please look after him for me and, when he is old enough to look after himself, please show him his hut in Ruga village." Nsia also left a two thousand shillings note.

Nkanambo had no choice but to raise the boy, but she always kept asking herself what had happened to Nsia and who was the father of her son. Nsia never disclosed anything to her and she was nowhere to answer her questions.

Nsia's first destination was Manga, a growing town near the Meremeta diamond mines. She lived there for five months and met a businesswoman; they became friends. One day *Mama Lao*[17] told Nsia that she should not continue living at Manga. "My dear, you are wasting your time here. Manga is not your place. I am taking you to Donga, the city of everything. You will prosper there, but not here." The woman took Nsia to Donga and gave her everything, including food, shelter, pocket money, and clothes.

After a few days, the woman introduced Nsia to her business in Donga. She was taken to a bar and restaurant. It was in a busy street, so it had customers all the time. "You will work here, my dear. You will serve customers. I am telling you – soon you will have your own bar or even a hotel. You just have to get used to

---

[16] Type of banana that is mainly grown in the Kilimanjaro region

[17] A nickname which is not a respectable title for a woman. Normally it is used in bars, guesthouses etc for businesswomen who keep girls for prostitution and those who sell local brews.

the principles of this work; get used to them and enjoy life."

Nsia did not understand what the principles of working in such a place were until a man called Rama followed her to her room one day after work. He told her that his visit was officially known by *Mama Lao*. "I know you are frightened, but do not worry. It won't hurt, Nsia," he told Nsia while undressing. She then understood what principles she had to get used to. It took Nsia days and months before she could accept the situation she was in. Every day a man would go to her room after bar hours. She would not give her body voluntarily, but they would take it by force.

She knew neither happiness nor love. Every day was full of sadness and pain. She one day asked *Mama Lao*, "What is the difference between pain and love?"

Mama Lao looked puzzled, but she at last answered her. "I can't tell about love because I have never experienced it. I only know how pain feels. We all face pain, Nsia, but we face it so we can live. It is not easy to find love in this world. Only a few men give love; many of them leave us with pain and nothing else. Anyway go to work. Customers will soon leave."

Two years passed and Nsia was still working for *Mama Lao*. She worked as a bar counter woman during the day and during the night she would stay in her room and wait for the customer of the day. Her business was under the control of *Mama Lao*. She would wait for male customers who went to her place looking for a woman to sleep with. Sometimes there would be more than one customer all wanting to sleep with Nsia. In that situation, Nsia had no other choice, but to sleep with each in turn.

She had learnt to hate her body and no longer found difficulty in spreading her legs before lustful men. She no longer felt pain as drunken men pressed harder to satisfy their ego. Hatred had taken the place of pain. She hated every man who paid to sleep with her. She could not see any difference between the day His Excellency Tupa raped her and the rest of the days she went to bed with other men.

To her, every single act was rape and all men were the same. She could see each man with the face, voice, and strength like that of His Excellency Tupa.

One thing that made her wonder was that most of the men who raped her were married. One of her regular customers was called Rama. He was a government official in a high position. He used to go to *Mama Lao's* place at 11pm when customers had started to leave the place so that he would not be seen. Rama was married and had four children: Three daughters and a son. Three of his children were studying in South Africa and the fourth in Canada. It was this man who took Nsia's life to another stage.

After being her customer for two years, Rama was able to persuade Nsia to leave *Mama Lao's* place. He rented a three roomed house for Nsia at the outskirts of the city. Nsia got everything she wanted from Rama. She wondered whether Rama had time to spend with his wife. She always felt partly responsible for other women's sufferings, but she did not know how to get out of that business. "I never look out for men, they come after me. If they stop coming, it will be the end of it," she told herself.

One day Nsia asked Rama about his wife. "What explanation do you give to your wife whenever you go home late?" she asked.

"No explanation. She is the mother of my children after all," Rama responded. He thought Nsia was worried that his wife would one day find them so he tried to assure her, "Do not ever think she will know about our affair. No need to worry darl…"

"Listen, Rama," she interrupted him, "do not ever think I am doing prostitution out of need for anything – Not out of need for love, money, cars, houses, clothes, gold, or prestige. I do not receive anything in exchange and I do not give anything either. I do not take someone's things, so I have nothing to fear, and I do not give anything away, so I have nothing to lose because for me nothing is of value anymore. It is you who should fear because you are giving too much of what you should give to your family to someone who does not deserve. You have taken everything away from your wife. I will not care if you do not come back to me again. I swear I will never cry because of it. I will be happy you have gone back to your wife and children. About me, do not worry. I ceased to live a long time ago. I no longer exist, Rama."

Ever since that day, Nsia never saw Rama again. It took her a few weeks to realise that she was pregnant. This time, she was not shocked. It was something she was expecting. She had had sex twice with two different men without using condoms. The first time it was with Rama. On that day, Rama had forgotten to buy condoms and Nsia had used hers with another man before Rama's turn. The second time it was with a man called Sakawa, another regular customer. On that day, they were both drunk and could not remember anything.

The only problem was that she could not know exactly who between Rama and Sakawa had impregnated her. Nine months passed and Nsia gave birth to a beautiful baby girl. One day she took her daughter in her arms and talked to her as if she could understand, "I am so sorry, my dear. Your mother does not exist, it is only her body. What a pity that, like your brother, you will never know or see your father. The days I became pregnant for you and your brother I never felt anything, but pain and grief, I was not making love, but being raped." Nsia wiped the tears from both her cheeks and she started to smile. "I will call you Sholanda, my Sholanda," she said and hugged her baby tightly.

Fourteen years passed and Nsia's life had deteriorated. She had stopped working as a prostitute. She and Sholanda lived with Kidude, a friend, in one room in a slum area. Kidude was still working as a prostitute, so she was sure of bringing food for the three of them. Sholanda remained home and looked after her mother. She was already in Form One but her attendance in school deteriorated day by day just like her mother's health. She never knew what disease her mother was suffering from, but everyday she witnessed her condition worsening.

One day Sholanda was outside their room pounding *kisamvu*[18] when her mother called from inside. Sholanda ran inside and kneeled before her mother. Nsia reached out for Sholanda's hand and pressed her tightly. "*Mwanangu mpendwa nimekuita nataka nikueleze jambo,*"[19] she said and coughed with pain and spit in a *kopo* filled with sand beside her. "What I want to tell you is very important, so you must listen and do as I say."

Sholanda looked worried. "Do not worry, Mama, I will do whatever you say," she assured her mother.

Nsia took an envelope from under a mat she was lying on and gave it to Sholanda. "Take this, my dear. In this envelope there are fifty five thousand shillings. I kept them for you from the day I realised I was pregnant. It is your savings. I want you to do the...cooh cooh cooh..." she coughed and spit before she continued. "You see I am sick and I will die soon, so I want you not to be like your mother, my dear. Never be like me. When I am gone, go to a village called Ruga. That is the village where I was born and raised. I left there twenty two years ago. Actually, I ran away. You must go, my dear. It is your true home. It is where you will find peace, love, and care. When you get to that village, ask for *Mzee Kundaeli*'s place. Whoever you ask will surely show you the place. Kundaeli was my father and my mother was Bilha. They both passed away when I was young. In your grandparents' place I am sure you will meet someone, your brother. You have a brother, my daughter. He is six years older than you. He is called Rumishaeli. I left him when he was two months old."

Sholanda started to weep. Her tears were uncontrollable.

"Stop crying, my dear. Everything is going to be all right; you will see. Now listen, my..." she forced herself to continue speaking.

[18] Cassava leaves, a common vegetable among Tanzanians.

[19] My dear child, I have called you because I have something to tell you.

She was in great pain. "Mama, please stop it, mama," Sholanda cried. Nsia stopped for awhile until she had accumulated enough strength to continue talking.

"I want you to go to the village and never come back to the city, my dear. When you meet your brother, tell him I am sorry. Ask him to forgive his mother because she could not take care of him. She ran away from him because she ceased to exist the day she was raped. Ouh ouh…also tell him about my illness and my death. Tell him..aah aah ouh…."

"Mama, mother, please mother, do not go. Please do not die mother. Motheeeeeeer…!" Nsia had been taken very far from Sholanda, very far from the mat she was lying on, very far from the room she was suffering in, indeed very far from the cruel world…!

PLAYS

"The Monster"

by Anna Chikoti

Characters:

Chitale and Mlonga, Two young men who are best of friends

Ladislai and Leseyo, Two wise and respected old men

Man, One of the victims

Woman, One of the villagers

Doctor

Patient

Teacher

Male host

Female host

Setting:

Village in Africa.

Scene 1

On stage, a group of people (men and women, old and young) are standing staring in different directions like they are looking for something. Suddenly the sound of a horrifying roar is heard. Everyone's attention is interrupted and they all look confused; some are looking for places to hide and a few are busy searching for where the sound comes from. Another roar is heard. They all run off stage. Two young men appear on stage right after the group leave. They have weapons on their shoulders.

Chitale: *[Runs to the middle of the stage breathing heavily.]* Did you hear that Mlonga?

Mlonga: *[Also breathing audibly.]* Yes, I did, but where is everyone?

The terrifying roar is now fading away.

Chitale: You are asking where they are. *[Chuckles]* We were always the first to reach the area whenever it attacked; nowadays we come when the fight is over.

Mlonga: You are right Chitale, we have always been the first to come out, but have you by any chance got a glimpse of the Monster on any of these days? I don't think so. So I do not see a reason why we should keep on being the first to come out.

Chitale: I think you have got a point there.

Mlonga: I know I do, I know I do my friend.

The two men leave the stage.

Scene 2

A very beautiful house decorated with white zigzag lines around its mud wall. Beautiful flowers all around. Two people (a man and a woman) are standing at either side of the door, all dressed up and looking smart. Both wear very inviting smiles on their faces. Two old men are standing a bit far from the house watching. Women and men are invited in the house in pairs. Men are received by the woman at the door and the women by the man. After a while, people are leaving the house coughing and in pain. They are unable to walk properly. A man leaves the house coughing just like the others and approaches the two old men.

Man: *[Coughing.]* I greet you, my elders.

Ladislai and Leseyo: *[In unison.]* We greet you, son.

Ladislai: *[Looking so concerned.]* What is the problem, my son? What is going on at that house? Everybody is coming out coughing and some don't leave at all.

Leseyo: Yes, son, tell us. Are you given food with too much pepper or are they poisoning you?

Man: *[Still coughing but trying very hard to speak.]* Pepper would have been the best thing compared to what is in that house. *[Blows his nose.]* Do you remember the Monster we have been hearing about lately? I tell you, elders, it is in that house. It lives in the tea prepared by that woman.

Ladislai: *[Surprised, looks at Leseyo, who looks back at him smiling.]* It cannot be, that beautiful house with a Monster, and it is the tea they prepare? Be serious, son; do not joke about something as serious as this. How can a big Monster live in a cup of tea?

Man: *[Leaving the old men while shouting.]* So you think I can joke with my elders? Well, how about you two go there and see for yourselves? *[Muttering to himself and coughing at the same time.]* Let them be cheated by the look of the house. Oh my, I wish I never took that sweet tea from the lady.

He disappears from the stage, leaving the two old men still looking at the house.

Ladislai: [*Looking at Leseyo now.*] Do you think he was telling the truth? Is there a Monster in that house or do they just not want us to go there and enjoy the tea?

Leseyo: [*Nodding his head.*] There must be something in that house because everyone coming from that house looks really sick. I do not think they are all pretending.

Ladislai: [*Nodding his head and looking at the other direction where two men can be heard moving towards them.*]

Chitale and Mlonga approach the two old men and argue about something. Their voices are heard, but in low volume.

Chitale: I told you that nobody knows where the Monster lives and you do not want to believe me. You just like to waste time.

Mlonga: [*Adjusting the swords and spears on his shoulder.*] Why don't you want to believe? You have heard it from more than ten people and even from those who visited the house. What more evidence do you want?

Nearing the old men they walk slowly and stop in front of Ladislai and Leseyo. They put their weapons down and look at the old men.

Chitale and Mlonga: [*In unison.*] We greet you, elders.

Leseyo and Ladislai: [*Also in unison.*] We greet you, sons.

Ladislai: What are you arguing about, my sons? Is it about the Monster? Because, I can see you are carrying your weapons ready to fight.

Chitale: [*Relief on his face.*] I was just trying to make Mlonga see reason. We have been searching for the Monster since I can remember, and some people came up with a story that the Monster lives in a very beautiful house with a man and a woman as hosts. Do you see how baseless it sounds? The worst part is my friend here believes the story.

Ladislai: [*Laughs a little.*] My son, it seems like you have given up the search for the Monster. It is true that the Monster lives in that house, just turn to your left and you will see the house.

Chitale and Mlonga at the same time turn to their left with a look of disbelief on their faces.

Mlonga: [*Says with awe.*] Ooh my God, have you ever seen such a beautiful house in your life, Chitale?

Chitale: [*Staring at the woman.*] Oh my! Have you ever seen such a beautiful face in all your life, Mlonga? She is a Goddess. I will sell my plot, house, wife, and children if that's what it takes to be invited into her house.

The two old men look at each other and cough a bit to regain Chitale and Mlonga's attention. The men are so embarrassed; they do not look the old men in the eyes.

Ladislai: Sons, do not be taken in by the beauty of the house or the woman. The Monster lives there. So what you have to do is go back to the people and tell them. We will discuss later about how to attack the house.

Leseyo: We are going to tell people not to go to that house until we find a solution on how to make the Monster disappear. Do not forget to send someone to town. The doctor should be called. Those people who have been attacked need treatment.

Ladislai: Yes, the doctor should be called and he should be told about the Monster. I heard that the Monster was in town before the people in town sent it to our village.

Chitale looks at the two old men, then at Mlonga, before looking back at the house.

Mlonga: [*Looks at Chitale warningly.*] Hey Chitale! You are not thinking about going to that house, are you? You heard it's dangerous. We have to do something and going there alone is out of the question.

Chitale: [Looks at the woman who smiles at him.] I was just thinking that I could convince the lady to let us kill the Monster. We do not have to be a team to convince one lady, do we?

Ladislai: [Looks at the house, very worried.] Of course we do not need an army to convince one lady, but it seems like everyone is taken in by her beauty. People lose their ability to reason whenever they come near the lady or the gentleman at her side.

Leseyo: [*Puts his hands on Chitale's shoulders and looks him in the eyes.*] We understand you son, but we need to sit down and talk about it deeply. Not only you young people, but also us, because the Monster does not choose its victims. We want to find the safest way to attack it without being scratched.

Chitale: Yes, of course, we will discuss it with everyone. Let us go and inform everyone about the meeting.

They all leave the stage, going different directions. The two old men leave together and Chitale and Mlonga also leave together.

Scene 3

Outside Ladislai's house. A round mud-walled, two-roomed house. White stripes pass around the mud wall in a zigzag fashion. People are sitting on mats and sacks. Others, who are much older, are sitting on chairs. Ladislai and Leseyo are sitting on chairs surrounded by the villagers. They all look sad, holding their faces in the palms of their hands.

Ladislai: [*Clears his throat.*] I greet you all. We all know why we are gathered here today. In case there are others who do not, we are faced by a terrible curse, something that has never happened before in our village. I do not know if it's something we have done against our God, but I know that we are vanishing one by one. I fear that at the end of the day no one will be here to give me drinking water.

Leseyo: Yes, it's a terrible curse and we have to do something as soon as possible. We cannot have a village without people and we need parents who will be there to shape our children. And do not forget that we, old people, need to be taken care of. So we all need to come together to fight this nameless Monster.

Ladislai: [*Stands up and starts moving around people, thinking.*] As an elder of this village, I have decided that both strong men and women should carry their weapons and go attack this Monster. We should wait until dark, so that it won't see us approaching. Then we will burn the house, everyone and everything in it.

Chitale: [*Waves his hands in the air, stands up and looks at Ladislai and Leseyo.*] Excuse me, elders.

Ladislai: [*Nods his heard in Chitale's direction.*] Yes, son, you seem like you have something very important to tell us. Go ahead.

Chitale: [*Bows.*] Thank you very much, my elders. My problem is, after burning that beautiful house, then what? I heard that, the people who have been attacked by the Monster can induce the curse to other people. What do we do with these people?

People start murmuring. Voices start so low, then increase until the murmur bursts into a whole lot of noise.

Leseyo: [*Clears his throat loudly. Voices fade away.*] We are not here to inculcate fear into people, but to solve the problem that faces us at present. If the people who have been attacked can attack other people, then we have to look for a possible and safe way to solve this other problem. Noise and fear will not solve the problems.

Ladislai: [*Nods his head.*] You are right, Leseyo, it will never solve the problems. So now we have two problems, the Monster and the people it has attacked. We do not have enough knowledge about the Monster. Before we plan anything, we need to know more about it so that we will know where to start. I sent for a doctor from town yesterday, I wonder why he has not arrived until now.

Woman: [*Stands up and tries to talk while crying.*] What do we need a doctor for? We have used every possible medicine in this village, starting from the roots of the tree to the highest leaves. Nobody has been cured. People are still sick, they are dying and others are still attacked by the Monster. If we have not succeeded in curing people by all the medicine we have, how is he going to do it?

Ladislai: [*Approaches the woman. He puts his hands on her shoulders.*] Sit down woman, crying will not help anything. If I decided to call a doctor, it's because he has greater knowledge of the Monster. He must know a lot about it, because the Monster started attacking people in town before coming here. We should expect something from him shouldn't we?

The woman sits down. People are nodding in agreement.

Leseyo: [*Clears his throat.*] We are going to wait for the doctor. Until then, nobody is allowed to take tea from the people who have been attacked.

From the other side of the stage a middle aged doctor approaches with a young man holding his bag. He is wearing a long white hospital coat and spectacles. He approaches the place where people are sitting.

Ladislai: [*Looking at the doctor.*] The doctor is here. First, we are going to listen to the doctor. Then we will know what to do.

The young man, who came with the doctor, goes to Ladislai's house and comes out with a chair and gives it to the doctor.

Doctor: *[Sitting down.]* Thank you, young man. I greet you all.

Ladislai: *[Looking at the doctor.]* Thank you for coming, Doctor. I am going to tell you briefly about why we have decided to call you, though I am sure you have found out from the boy we sent. A Monster, nobody has seen its face and nobody is sure about its origin, has invaded our village. All we know is, it comes from town. It really scares us, Doctor. Our people are dying and we don't even have hospitals where they can be treated.

Leseyo: Yes, we are really scared, Doctor. When this Monster attacks a person, physical changes are noticed. The person becomes really sick. We have tried all the medicine in our village with no success. Can you do something, Doctor?

Doctor: *[Clears his throat.]* Thank you for trusting me. I am going to be as quick and honest as possible. It is true that we are facing this Monster in town. We have tried everything; have done research in all medications, but until now we have failed to find a cure. In all the beautiful houses, you will find it, as well as stones which have been used in grinding ginger. This is the spice which is put in tea in those houses. And if a person is attacked by this Monster, that person can also infect others.

Chitale: *[Anger in his voice.]* We know all that, Doctor. What we want is for you to treat those people who have been attacked and tell us how to kill the Monster once and for all.

Doctor: That is why I am here, young man. I just wanted you to know that I understand perfectly what you are talking about, that we both are in the same boat. First, I would like to see those who have been attacked. Second, do not go near their houses and never drink their tea. I have heard about how sweet that tea is, but we can always have tea in our own houses. Tea in your own houses is very safe unless, of course, the one who boils it has been attacked by the Monster.

Mlonga: Should we isolate the people who have been attacked? Since no one knows when they will come after you, it's better to put them away for good.

Doctor: [*Chuckles.*] Even if you decide to put them away, which I wouldn't advise, you can never be sure who has been attacked just by looking at them. It will be very difficult to isolate them. One thing I am sure is that most of them scratch you when you go willingly to them, they rarely do it by force. So it's up to you not to be scratched. Try to give the victims a sense of belonging; then, they will also be good to us. They are our brothers and sisters after all. But, stay as far away from the house as possible.

Chitale: We have already decided to burn that house down, Doctor, and everyone in it, including the Monster. That way we will kill the Monster and get rid of its curse.

They nod their heads seemingly in agreement with Chitale.

Doctor: I told you before that the Monster doesn't die that easily. Actually it doesn't die at all, for now you know only one house. Do you think it's the only one with the Monster? No, a lot of houses have the Monster, only that they are not marked for you to see. All I am asking is for you to stay as far away from the house as possible. Drink tea only from your own houses. It is everyone's responsibility to make sure that the boiled tea is enough for a household, so that no one will be tempted to go out for more tea.

Everyone stands up; the doctor goes inside Ladislai's house. There's a chair near the fireplace where he sits. The attacked victims go in, and come out with fruits, vegetables, and water. But still with long faces.

Doctor: [*Looking at one of the patients.*] I am giving you fruits, vegetables and water, so that you will be kept strong for the time being. Another thing you need to have for your survival is hope. That will make your days brighter with a lot of opportunity.

Patient: [*Coughing, shouts at the doctor.*] And how much time do we have, Doctor? And you want us to have hope. What for? Death? You know what; we are just wasting our time here.

The patient storms out of the room, leaving everyone in Ladislai's house astonished. The doctor stands up, shakes hands with the patients and goes out of the house. People are outside waiting and they all escort the doctor off the stage.

Scene 4

Outside the Monster's house, another day, the sun is setting. People are still going in and out. Some are leaving the house completely, while others are exchanging roles with the hosts at the door and remain standing at the door in pairs. It goes on for two minutes, with different hosts standing at the door in turn. Chitale, Mlonga, and a few villagers are standing a mile away from the house looking at it amazed. Everyone is carrying a weapon ready to attack; others are carrying kerosene and lighted sticks. Ladislai and Leseyo are seen approaching very slowly with sticks. They see the villagers standing near the beautiful house. They try to quicken their steps, approaching the villagers.

Ladislai: [*Breathing hard and coughing a little, looks at the villagers one by one, then his eyes rest on Chitale. He clears his throat.*] What is this? [*Chitale and a few of the villagers look down.*] I am asking what is going on here? Did we not agree that we will stay away from that house? [*Pointing at the beautiful house with his stick, he then looks at the villagers one by one.*]

When will all of you understand that it's better this way? Were you not at the meeting with the doctor?

Chitale: [*Looks at Ladislai's face.*] We are sorry that we didn't inform you of our new decision. We have decided to burn the house. We will isolate everybody who has been attacked by the Monster. We have built a special house for them in the mountains where they will stay until they die.

Ladislai: [*Shakes his head in disappointment.*] And who are you to decide? The final decision was reached at the meeting. We did not allow for aftermath decisions, did we? My children, if you don't know something, accept it and at least try to listen to those who know. Only two days ago, the doctor came and now you have forgotten everything he said.

Chitale: It is not that I am being disrespectful, but nobody here knows if what the doctor said is true. He could be lying for all we know. Anyway, we have decided not to take any chances.

Ladislai: [*Looking even more disappointed, he looks at Leseyo.*] What do you think, Leseyo?

Leseyo: [*Smokes his cigar for sometime, then throws it on the ground grinding it with his worn out shoes, then looks at Ladislai.*] I agree with you, Ladislai, it is better we listen to those who know. [*He turns around to look at the villagers.*] Why waste your energy on something which you cannot destroy by your arrows and knives? But we can control it, can't we? It's better you lose yourselves in your work. The sweet tea from the Monster's house will be the last thing in your minds. We have asked for a teacher from Kikungu village to come and tell us more about the Monster. We need to be in our right mind to fight the Monster. So I do not see the reason why you should waste your time here.

The villagers shake their heads in disagreement; everyone tries to talk until it becomes noisy.

Ladislai: [*Clears his throat noisily. Everyone stops talking at once and looks at Ladislai. He says gently.*] Noise is never the solution. As your elder, I order you to wait for the teacher and listen to what he says.

The teacher approaches with books in his hands and a pen in his shirt pocket. One of the villagers runs to help him with his books. He wears very neat trousers and a clean but worn jacket.

Teacher: [*Coming straight to the group of villagers and looking at Ladislai and Leseyo.*] I greet you, elders.

Ladislai: We greet you, son. Thank you for coming, Teacher. As you have heard this unknown Monster attacks us. People die every day. Look at the house on your right. [*He points his forefinger at the beautiful house.*] Everyone seems to like tea from that house more than what is prepared in their homes, and because they cannot overcome the temptation, they want to destroy the house. What do you think, Teacher?

Leseyo: [*Clears his throat.*] Before we listen to the teacher's opinion, are we going to talk right here? I thought it would be better to go to the house, it's getting dark already.

Ladislai: [*Thinks for a moment.*] You have a point there, Leseyo, but I think it is better we speak right here, where people can see what we are talking about. Because the teacher is going to sleep in our village today, there is no need of rushing. We better sit on this grass and listen to the teacher.

They all find places to sit. The teacher takes a piece of cloth from his pocket, spreads it and sits on it. Others try to find places around the teacher. Everyone makes sure that he sits where he can see the teacher.

Teacher: [*Takes one of his books and reads it for a while before turning to the villagers.*] This Monster has now spread to almost every village. I have been to seven villages and they are all complaining about the Monster. No body until now has been lucky enough to see its face or shape.

A terrifying sound is heard from afar. Villagers cling to each other, so scared, and they move even closer to the teacher. A few of them are courageous enough to take out their weapons.

Teacher: Do not be scared, people. The Monster does not attack unless you go willingly to it. So imagine that sound, you can hear it from miles away, but the Monster lives in that sweet tea. Isn't that enough reason for us to stay away from its tea, no matter how sweet it is? Look around yourselves, look closely at your neighbour's faces and tell me what you see.

People start to look at each other's faces; they turn to their neighbours on the right, left, behind and in front. They all look confused.

Chitale: Well, I don't see anything strange. All I see is faces I have seen all my life.

Teacher: [*Nods his head.*] Exactly. The faces you have known all your life. Do you think because you have seen those faces all your life, it's a guarantee that you can tell if they have been attacked by the Monster or not? No, my friends, that's wrong. By the time you realise that they have been attacked by the Monster, it will be too late.

The villagers look again at each other, but this time with doubt written on their faces.

Teacher: I didn't say that these people here have been attacked. All I say is, it is so difficult to tell if one of us has been attacked, because there is no mark that says so.

Chitale: [*Looks like he is going to cry any minute.*] So, what shall we do, Teacher? We need to live a life that is full of peace. We don't like the life full of fear, the life of looking over our shoulders every second. Please, Teacher, tell us how many cows are needed for sacrifices.

The villagers look worried and they nod in agreement at what Chitale says.

Teacher: There is no better sacrifice to destroy the Monster than ourselves. No number of cows or sheep can chase away the Monster. If all of us stick together and sacrifice ourselves, then the Monster will live, but not in us.

Chitale: *[Shocked, horror on his face. He shakes his head from side to side in disbelief.]* What!? You want us to sacrifice ourselves? Now I believe that the Doctor is better than this Teacher. If we are to sacrifice ourselves, isn't it the same as going to drink that sweet tea, which I would rather do.

Teacher: *[Looks at the confused faces of the villagers.]* You didn't understand what I was saying. I didn't mean that you sacrifice yourselves the way you do with cows and sheep. By sacrifice, I meant we all leave our differences aside and work for the same goal, making sure that the Monster loses the battle. How will you feel, when at last you see the Monster looking down with shame because of losing the battle?

Villagers: *[Nod their heads and shout very loudly.]* Yes! Yes! Yes! The Monster has to bow to us. We are going to shame it.

Chitale: *[Speaks loudly above the voices of the villagers.]* But what exactly should we do, Teacher?

Teacher: *[Suddenly seized by a lighthearted mood.]* This voice that belongs to all of you is enough to shame the devil. This unity you have shown me here should be induced in every villager. Each of you is a protector of the other. Do not let anyone of you go for that sweet tea, because all of you can do without it. And for those who have been attacked, the best way to overcome grief is to hope. Be optimistic and each one of you has a responsibility of insuring that victims have that sense of belonging.

71

Because you are united, it does not mean that the victims are not a part of us anymore; after all it's because of them that we are united right? Well, that's all I have to say.

Everyone cheers up. They all stand and jump up and down watching the beautiful house. The hosts at the beautiful house look worried, the male host turns to the female host.

Male host: [*Horror registered on his face.*] Do you think they are going to win?

Female host: [*Also looks worried.*] Do you think with that determination, we will defy them this time? I don't think so. Still, let's hope that a few of them will be so pig headed as not to listen.

They enter into the house and close the door behind them.

Ladislai: [*Standing up from the piece of wood where he was sitting so slowly and groaning loudly, hands at his waist as if in pain.*] I think it's late, we better get moving now that we have reached a conclusion. Thank you, Teacher; we really appreciate your presence today. You have made us see that it's always so easy to give up, but it is so costly.

Leseyo: [*Shakes hands with the Teacher.*] Thank you, Teacher. We really need a lot of people like you in this village as well as in other villages. We welcome you again in our village anytime, it's your home, come visit us again. Do not wait for another Monster to attack us before you visit.

Teacher: [*Smiles.*] Thank you so much. I will come again sometime soon. And even if another Monster comes, there will be no problem because I believe that together we can destroy anything that invades us.

The villagers throw their weapons down and start leaving the stage while singing.

Villagers: [*Singing.*]

    We have gone a long way.
    We have suffered great deal.
    We have searched very far,
    Worked, with no avail.

    The people of great wisdom,
    The doctors of great experience,
    The world of highest technology,
    Worked, with no avail.

    Let bygones be bygones.
    Let's face today when it's still today.
    We do not know what the future will hold,
    But we are aware of what is in today.

    Watch out now for the so called friend.
    We are going to pay you a visit,
    Only this time officially.
    We know now more than ever.

Voices fade away.

"Love is…"

by Kimberley McLeod

Characters:

April, a 27 year old from New Jersey
Isaac, a 29 year old from Georgia
Reverend Elijah Jacob Wilkins, Isaac's 57 year old father
Sister Mary Elizabeth Wilkins, Isaac's 52 year old mother
Wedding Guests, close friends and family

Setting:

Savannah, Georgia (USA)

Scene 1

The lights are out and the stage appears empty. The sounds of church organs and exalting grow, then subside, as the Rev. Wilkins begins giving a sermon. It is Thanksgiving Day.

Rev. Wilkins: [*Offstage.*] See the Bible says, "Be ye not unequally yoked." "Be ye *not* unequally yoked together with unbelievers: for what fellowship hath righteousness with unrighteousness? And what communion hath light with darkness?" Christ ain't got nothing to do with Satan, so what business you got with an unbeliever? ["Halleujah!"] Yea. Say, yea. ["Yea!"] It say, "Wherefore come out from among them, be ye separate, saith the Lord, and touch not the unclean thing." You hear me? ["Reverend, we hear ya!"] Imma say it again, "Touch *not* the unclean thing." You know why? ["Tell us Reverend! Tell us!"] Cos if you touch something unclean, it'll dirty you up. Make ya unclean too! It say it right here…II Corinthians 6:14. I don't know about you but I wanna stay clean. I don't know about you but I –

As the voice fades, the lights come up. There is a large mahogany dining table with eight chairs. A crystal chandelier hangs from the middle of the room. On stage right a wooden staircase leads upstairs. Isaac is placing plates on the table. April enters from stage right and comes down the stairs smiling.

April: [*Whispers.*] Well, good morning you. [*April grabs Isaac from behind and tries to kiss him. Startled, Isaac grabs April's hands and gives her a peck on the cheek. April frowns.*]

April: [*Looks towards the kitchen and speaks loudly.*] Last night was –

Isaac: [*Covers her mouth, kisses her lips with his eyes open and glued on the doorway.*] Shh…not so loud. They'll hear you.

April: [*Whispers.*] Last night was incredible. I knew you'd be pleased with how "light" I packed. [*Laughs.*] I bought

75

a new pair for *every* night we spend at your parents' house!

Isaac: April! [*Still staring at the kitchen, pulls her down into the chair next to him.*]

April: What? Babe, it's been five years. [*Looks at the labels on the sparkling cider bottles.*] Do you really think your parents are clueless? [*Gets up and starts searching cabinets for a bottle of wine and reads all the labels.*]

They only make us sleep in separate rooms because they're in denial.

Isaac: Naw, Mama is pretty convinced.

April: [*Frustrated, slams the cabinet doors.*] And who exactly convinced her?

Isaac: Sweety, you know how she feels about fornication.

April: [*Imitating Isaac*] Fornication. [*Groans and sits.*] You make it sound so biblical and sinful...so...dirty! [*Smiles.*]

Isaac: [*Begins to stand.*] Jesus!

April: [*Pulling him back down.*] Relax. No need to summon Jesus. I'm just tired of keeping up appearances, Isaac. Five years I've had to pretend to be something I'm not. I'm not the little saved and baptized, saw the light at the end of the tunnel, holy ghost fulfilled and "saintified" thirteenth disciple your parents want to believe I am.

Isaac: I've never asked you to pretend. Just to be...discrete.

April: But we're getting *married*.

Isaac: I know, I know...just give it some time.

April: Time? I think we should just tell them tonight.

Isaac: We are going to tell them tonight.

April: Isaac. Not just the engagement. About...our amazing night last night, the even more amazing one I intend on having tonight, and many, many, many more nights *before* our wedding…about the fact that the only prayer I know is "Now I Lie Down and Sleep."

Isaac: [*Laughs and shakes his head.*] Mama has waited for this day practically all my life…shoot, practically all *her* life. I'm not trying to ruin the news of our engagement with anything else.

April: Ruin? Well, I'm sorry if I left my comfortable life…left my family, friends, worked my behind off for years, then risked losing *all* I had worked for to move in with *you*, all for the sake of tainting the holy image Mother Theresa and the Pope have of me!

Isaac: I promise you; we will tell my parents. No more hiding. [*Pulls April onto his lap.*] Just not tonight.

Rev. Wilkins and Sis. Wilkins' voices become more audible as they approach the dining room. Isaac quickly shoves April into her seat and she almost falls off. April sighs. Lights fade.

Scene 2

Rev. Wilkins and Sis. Wilkins enter from stage left. Sis. Wilkins is carrying a stuffed turkey, while Rev. Wilkins is sharpening the carving knife.

Rev. Wilkins: [*Laughs heartily.*] Now *that's* a pretty looking bird! If I may say so myself.

Sis. Wilkins: You may *not* say so yourself, cuz you ain't the one that cook this bird, right here.

Isaac: Mama, that turkey does look mighty fine. I have to agree with Pops.

April: Yes, Mrs. Wilkins, everything looks delicious.

Sis. Wilkins: Why thank you sugar! And how was your night dear?

April: It was probably one of the best nights I've had since I've moved from Jersey. I was just telling Isaac about it. [*Turns to Isaac.*] Why don't you tell your mom how you slept, hunny? [*Smiles innocently.*]

Isaac: Uhh...great Mama. Can't complain. [*Gives April a stern look.*] Thanks for ironing my jamies last night, Ma; they were extra...crisp. [*April tries to suppress laughter.*] Oh, sweetheart didn't you want to thank Mom for the Bible she left on your nightstand? April left her copy at home... I don't know how she woulda functioned.

April: Oh yes, how could I forget? [*Kicks Isaac under the table.*] Thank you.

Rev. Wilkins: I don't mean to interrupt you folks and your fine conversation, but "Watch ye and pray, lest ye enter into temptation. The spirit truly is ready, but flesh is weak."

Isaac: [*Shouts quickly.*] Mark chapter 14 verse 37!

Sis. Wilkins: Nope! Verse 38! Gotcha! [*Everyone bursts into laughter except April.*]

Rev. Wilkins: [*Laughs.*] This bird sure is tempting; not just my spirit but my *belly* is ready and it's weak I tell you! [*Laughs.*]

Sis. Wilkins. Alright, Goliath. Sit! [*Turns to April.*] April, sugar, why don't you lead us in grace, dear?

April: Aw, that's very sweet of you. And...I'm honored but uh...I think Isaac should lead us. He always does such a good job.

Rev. Wilkins: Now don't be shy, April. You're practically the fourth member of this family. Just let the grace of God guide you and the words will come.

Isaac: Yea, sweety, just let the grace of God guide you. [*Chuckles lightly.*]

April: [*Clears throat.*] Alrighty. [*Takes a deep breath.*] Glorious God...we give our praise to this...glorious meal –

Sis. Wilkins: Yes Lord, yes Lord.

April: And for the turkey –

Rev. Wilkins: Hallelujah!

April: And cornbread –

Rev. Wilkins: Hallelujah!

April: That will…fill our bodies…and our souls.

Rev. Wilkins: Bless his name.

April: Eh, we ask your gloriousness to spread…all over us today and make us full with your goodness and power and glory. Forever and forever. From ashes…to ashes and dust to dust –

Sis. Wilkins:. Praise his –

April: In the name of the Father, the Mother and the Son… Amen.

April looks up to find that everyone's eyes are already open and they are staring at her.

Isaac: Eh, Amen.

Rev. Wilkins: Well, then. Thank you for that…that…well, for that…[*Stands and picks up craving knife.*] [*Aside.*] Whatever it was!

Isaac: [*Laughs awkwardly.*] I don't know about yall, but I'm hungry. Let's eat!

Rev. Wilkins: Let the church say, "Amen!" [*Laughs loudly and begins serving turkey.*] You know, April, in these past five years, I don't think you've ever come to one church service. Come to think of it you've always had some conflict or had to head back to New Jersey before Sunday. [*Passes them their plates.*] Last Sunday the Holy Spirit was live and well among our youth. Sister Wilkins here has done a fine job filling them up with the Blood of the Lamb and has them yearning for more. Hallelujah!

April: That's wonderful. [*Drinks.*]

Sis. Wilkins: Actually, April, dear, tomorrow night is Youth Friday. I'm sure all the young people would love to meet you, pumpkin. In fact… [*Serves yams.*] I think you should help me lead Bible study.

Rev. Wilkins: That's a great idea, Sister Wilkins! What topic has God placed in your heart?

Sis. Wilkins. Abstinence. "When lust hath conceived, it bringeth forth sin: and sin, when it is finished bringeth forth death." James chapter 1 verse 15! [*Talks in tongues.*]

Isaac: Eh, Mama, whatchu put in this stuffing?

Sis. Wilkins: I could tell you son, but then I'd have to crucify you! [*Laughs.*] Now April, don't you see how God has blessed this family? Put a roof over our heads, given us tenfold what we could ask for? "If ye shall ask anything in my name, I will do it." Hallelujah. Don't you agree dear? [*April smiles awkwardly.*] Kinda like you and that job of yours. You and Isaac were so worried you'd lose your position when you moved to Atlanta, but by the grace of God, He blessed you with a promotion in their Georgia office! "And they said, Believe in the Lord Jesus Christ, and thou shalt be saved, and thy house."

Rev. Wilkins: Acts 16:31!

Isaac: Mama, April also worked very hard for that promotion.

Sis. Wilkins: I bet she did, sweet pea, but hard work means nothing without Jesus! "For whosoever shall call upon the name of the Lord shall be saved." Romans chapter 10 verse 13. April agrees, don't cha sugar?

April: No.

Sis. Wilkins: Excuse me?

April: I don't agree. I think you all are good people that have worked hard for what you've got. You've done right by others and people have done right by you in return. As for myself, I've worked for all that I have. I've never had to ask anyone for anything. My company promoted me because they know I'm responsible and capable of leading the firm. I've proved that for seven years. I don't believe some ghost or spirit in the sky did it *for* you or me.

Rev. Wilkins, Sis. Wilkins and Isaac are speechless.

April: Now if you'd excuse me for a moment. [*Gets up and walks towards stairs.*] Oh, and Isaac and I are getting married next September. [*Exits.*]

Lights fade.

Scene 3

There is a long awkward silence. Sis. Wilkins is forcefully cutting away at the turkey on her plate and begins to scrape the knife against the plate. The sound gets louder and louder.

Isaac: Mama.

Sis. Wilkins continues.

Isaac: Mama!

Sis. Wilkins: [*Stops.*] Isaac you are *not* going to marry that girl.

Isaac: Mama, like April told y'all. We plan to get married next year. [*Stands and walks over to Sis. Wilkins' chair.*] Ma, you love April. You and Pops, you both love her...why should tonight change anything?

Rev. Wilkins: [*Gets up.*] It changes everything, son.

Isaac: [*Points to Sis. Wilkins*] You, you told me how much you admired her—her upbringing, her loyalty. Mama, April has stood by me through it all...and I mean through it *all*. She's been my rock –

Sis. Wilkins: God's been your rock. Not that Anti-Christ you want to make your wife. I don't care if she had to raise her

81

four brothers and sisters since she was thirteen because her mother had to work three jobs before she died of a stroke. I don't care if she waited for you to figure out what you wanted to do with your life…backing you financially through law school, then seminary school, then law school again. I don't care!

Isaac: Mama, who was the first person to fly down here when the hurricane destroyed the church clinic? April got here before Pops did and he was just one town over! Dad, you remember? April was the one that organized the medical supplies drive.

Sis. Wilkins: All that don't matter without God!

Rev. Wilkins: Son, your mother is right. How can you possibly have a healthy marriage with someone who doesn't share something that is so fundamental to who you are… something that is at your very core.

Isaac: My faith might be at my core but it's not *who* I am.

Sis. Wilkins: Father Lord! I rebuke the devil's presence in this house.

April enters and stands at the top of the stairs.

Isaac: [*Sits beside Sis. Wilkins and takes her hand.*] You know what April and I share. [*Sis. Wilkins pulls her hand away and walks to the end of the table.*] "Wherefore they are no more twain, but one flesh…" [*Sis. Wilkins drops on her knees and begins to pray out loud.*] "What therefore God hath joined together" – [*Sis. Wilkins prays louder.*] "Let no man put asunder." Mathew chapter 19 verse 6.

Rev. Wilkins: How can you quote the Bible to defend what you two share when only *one* of you believes in it?!

April: He's right. We are one. [*Everyone turns to look at April as she walks down the stairs. Sis. Wilkins stops praying abruptly. She and Rev. Wilkins return to their seats. There is an awkward silence.*]

April: [*Resumes eating.*] Mmm. [*Talks with mouth full.*] These yams are delicious! You have to give me the recipe.

Sis. Wilkins: For some reason, I've lost my appetite.

Rev. Wilkins: [*Stands and walks over to April with water pitcher in hand. He acts if he is going to refill her glass with water, but dips his hand in the pitcher and tries to anoint April.*] In the name of Jesus, I command you Satan to leave this child. Huh! I command you devil to exit this body. In the name of Jesus! [*Presses his hand against April's forehead.*]

Isaac: Dad!

Rev. Wilkins: Father, huh, I ask, huh, that you save her.

Sis. Wilkins: Hallelujah! Hallelujah!

Rev. Wilkins: Show her you're the only way Lord! Show her Lord! Huh!

Isaac: [*Gets up and grabs April.*] We're leaving! [*Chair falls over.*] We'll be back tomorrow for our things

April: [*Nonchalantly.*] Thank you for dinner. It was lovely, really —

Rev. Wilkins: How can you marry our son before a god you don't even believe in?

April: I may not believe in your god, but I believe in love [*Looks at Isaac.*] and commitment.

Isaac: Come on, April.

Isaac and April walk towards exit. April stops.

April: For *five* years I've respected your beliefs. I only ask that you respect mine.

Isaac and April exit. Lights fade.

Scene 4

The majority of the food is still on the table and plates. A chair is still knocked over on the floor along with the water pitcher and April's plate of food.

Rev. Wilkins: [*Picks up the chair.*] Can you believe those two? I believe in love and commitment? These young folk today...when was love and commitment ever enough to sustain a marriage?!

Sis. Wilkins: [*Slowly scrapes leftovers into one place.*] I tell ya.

Rev. Wilkins: Love and commitment! Come in here eating all this good food [*Stuffs some leftover turkey in mouth.*] and wanna bring all that Satan talk in our home...in our *family*! I told you there was something funny about all that mascara she wore. For all we know — [*Sis. Wilkins gets up and walks to kitchen with plates.*] [*Speaking louder.*] Imagine our grandchildren! Little mascara wearing... devil worshippers!

Sis. Wilkins reenters with a rag in hand. Sits.

Rev. Wilkins: [*Walks over to Sis. Wilkins and massages her shoulders.*] Can you picture it? [*Laughs.*] Little mascara wearing tots running all over the house in diapers tearing the pages outta the Bible, breaking crosses in half!

Sis. Wilkins: Eyeliner.

Rev. Wilkins: What?

Sis. Wilkins: She wears eyeliner.

Rev. Wilkins: Mascara, eyeliner...magic marker. Same difference. [*Laughs.*] [*Sis. Wilkins looks away disinterested. Rev. Wilkins sits beside here.*] What's troubling you, Mary?

Sis. Wilkins: July 14ᵗʰ 1977. I remember it clearer than yesterday. The Bargain Bug down the street had just opened that weekend and just two hours before you picked me up I ran over there and picked out the most beautiful canary yellow dress. Had the shoes to match and everything. Spent *hours* that morning on my hair…straightening and curling…spraying and teasing.

Rev. Wilkins: I remember. You were quite a sight! Almost capsized when I saw you sitting on your porch waiting.

Sis. Wilkins: Then we walked over to this very house. Your Mama opened the door and by the look on her face, I thought she didn't like the dress! Or thought my hair was too much…I thought maybe they wanted a simpler girl for their son. I was fiddling all night. [*Looks hard at Rev. Wilkins now.*] Until your father reached home from work. From the look on *his* face I knew it didn't matter what kind of dress I wore or how I had done my hair. [*Rev. Wilkins looks away.*] None of that mattered. The way he asked, "*What* do we have here?" and called your big brother down to see "what" you brought home…I knew that my black skin would never be enough for their "bougy" lifestyle. Wouldn't even touch me…like I was dirty or something. [*Pauses and looks around the room.*] You could imagine my surprise when they chose you, their youngest child, and left this house in *both* our names. Yea, I remember it clearer than yesterday. Do you?

Rev. Wilkins: Yea, I remember.

Sis. Wilkins: So then you must remember what it felt like to have your parents reject the woman you chose to spend the rest of your life with.

Rev. Wilkins: It's not the same thing. [*Gets up and exits.*]

Sis. Wilkins stands and wipes the table. She stops, looks around the house, smiles, and turns out the light.

Scene 5

The dining table is gone. Along the staircase are white flowers. A white trail runs along the steps and on the wooden floor. The eight dining chairs are upstage right and arranged in two rows diagonally facing downstage left. The wedding guests, who include April's siblings and close friends and family of the bride and groom, are taking their seats. Sis. Wilkins and Isaac are standing on stage left. Sis. Wilkins hums as April is escorted down the stairs by Rev. Wilkins. When April arrives, Sis. Wilkins begins to sing "Still My Child."

Sis. Wilkins: [*Sings.*] *The next time you talk to God,*
   Would you please mention my name?
   Oh, tell Him that I really love Him,
   I know it's been a while.
   Ask Him for me, Am I still His Child.

[*Sis. Wilkins takes Isaac's hand, singing.*]
   I know the answer to your question.
   Yes, the Father still loves you.
   But sometimes when you have children
   you don't always like what they do.
   So when you go to your Heavenly Father say, Lord, I love you.
   And when you ask Him for forgiveness,
   this is what he'll say to you:
   I sent a message in the wind when the birds sang a song
   And when you went to sleep last night, I told the moon,
   Shine all night long.
   Just wanted you to talk to me and I know it's been a while
   And to answer your question,

[*Takes April's hand.*] *you are still my child.*

[*Joins both Isaac's and April's hands.*]

Rev. Wilkins: Dearly Beloved, we are gathered here today to join these two together in holy…and humanly matrimony.

86

[*Smiles.*] You know, the Bible says, "Love is patient, love is kind. It does not envy, it does not boast, it is not proud. [*Wedding guests shout praises throughout his sermon.*] It is not rude, it is not self-seeking, it is not easily angered, it keeps no record of wrongs." Halleujah! "Love does not delight in evil, but rejoices with the truth. It always protects, always trusts, always hopes, always perseveres. Love never fails."

Isaac: [*Quietly.*] First Corinthians chapter 13 verses 4 to 8.

Rev. Wilkins: [*Nods approvingly.*] What it does *not* say is that love is exclusive or that love is judgmental or "invite only." It ain't a mail-your-application-in-and-it'll-get-back-to-ya-in-two-to-three-weeks kinda love. [*Wedding guests laugh.*] We are *all* capable and worthy of such a love—regardless of what we've gone through, regardless of how much money we have, the shade of our skin, the religion we belong to…or don't belong to. [*Wedding guests begin to mumble. Rev. Wilkins speaks louder.*] What the Bible does *not* say is that you gotta…you gotta meet some kinda criteria to generate this kinda love. Naw. "… clothe yourselves with compassion…kindness, humility, gentleness and patience. Bear with each other and forgive whatever grievances you may have against one another." [*Looks at April.*] "Forgive as the Lord forgave you. And over all these virtues put on love, which binds them all together in perfect unity."

Sis. Wilkins and **Isaac:** [*Softly.*] Colossians Chapter 3 verses 12-14.

Rev. Wilkins: Sometimes we try to dig…dig *deep* into a person to find something that makes them different from us… different and undeserving of our love and acceptance, when right on the surface, through their actions, through their compassion, kindness, humility, gentleness and patience, we find that they are more than worthy. [*Looks at April and Sis. Wilkins.*] Yes! [*Laughs deeply.*] First Corinthians 13:4-8: "Love is patient, love is kind" but also love is respect and commitment. Love is these two. [*To Isaac.*] Love was your mother and I twenty-nine years ago and twenty-nine years later. April, ten months ago you showed me that I had forgotten that. You have been a part of our family ever since the day Isaac came home asking for money to take you out cause he was broke like joke in those days and still broke —

Isaac: Pop!

Rev. Wilkins: [*Clears throat.*] April, I don't want you to be the young woman fiddling with the hem on her dress and adjusting her hair all night cause she ain't think she was good enough. I want you to be my daughter-in-law, complete and whole, just as you are, and yes, before a god you don't believe in. Because in the end it's the same love that binds us together...as one.

April: Thank you.

Rev. Wilkins: Do you Isaac Emanuel Wilkins take April Zayna Johnson to be your lawfully wedded wife?

Isaac: I do.

Rev. Wilkins: Do you April Zayna Johnson take Isaac Emanuel Wilkins to be your lawfully wedded husband?

April: Hell, yeah. [*Wedding guests gasp.*] I mean, absolutely.

Rev. Wilkins: In that case, I now pronounce you husband and wife. You may kiss your beautiful bride.

Isaac and April kiss. Everyone cheers. April throws bouquet. ISSAC picks her up and they exit. Everyone soon follows the bride and groom out, applauding. A few moments pass, then April's voice is heard.

April: [*Offstage.*] I got them sweety. I got them! [*Stumbles onstage laughing. Stops. Looks around the house and smiles. She picks up car keys and turns out the lights.*]

"A Tanzanian Rooftop"

by Benjamin Branoff

Characters:

Bob, a southern American farm boy from Alabama. He always wears his Alabama ball cap with jeans and a t-shirt. He talks normal in normal conversations but gets excited in arguments. He has a significant beard.

Kirby, a friend of Bob's from back home. They've traveled together for their semester abroad. She's very pretty, very outgoing, and speaks her mind.

Belle, a French foreign exchange student. Very fair young lady. She has been studying Kiswahili. She wears colorful clothing with headbands and such in her wavy, long, dirty blond hair.

Dash, a French man also studying Kiswahili. He's clean-shaven but wears long hair.

Sam, a Tanzanian student staying in the international dormitory. He's fairly short, wears jeans and t-shirts, Rastafarian bracelets, a goatee, and likes to drink.

Salli, much like Sam but taller. Speaks with a slight lisp and more softly.

Shuji, a Japanese foreign exchange student. Knows fairly good English and is learning Kiswahili. He loves other languages and sometimes uses their words with extra passion.

Ralph, another American student. He's from New York City but shares the same thoughts as Bob.

Setting:

The rooftop of an international dormitory at the University of Dar es Salaam in Tanzania.

The sun beats heavily on the black tar roof of the international dormitory. In the middle of the roof and the middle of the stage, a small enclosure sits where the stairs exit from below and where clotheslines are strung. The exit from the stairs faces the audience, but can't be seen by those on stage right. In stage right sits the outer, eastside wall of this enclosure and a bench sits against the wall. One of its legs is missing. To compensate, that side rests on an old, partially rusted, metal chair. If the chair is removed, the bench is useless.

Trees flank the far sides of the roof, but the suburbs and the airport are clearly visible to the South, behind the stage. Through a break in the trees, the ocean can be seen to the East, to stage right.

Two new American students emerge onto the open roof from the staircase for the first time. They begin to walk around and explore.

Bob: Ahhh! Can you feel it Kirb? We're in Africa!

Kirby: I know, Bob. This is great. Africa, man. Africa! Tanzania! This is our new home, our home away from home.

Bob: Yea, 10,000 miles away. Just think, two days ago we were home and now we are here in Africa, in The Heart of Darkness. But I'm glad we came together, Kirb. This way, no matter what happens, we'll have each other. When the shit hits the fan, we'll have each other. Right?

Kirby: Yea, Ben, we have each other.

Bob: Good.

Kirby: Wow! It's gorgeous. I still can't believe we're here. It's so beautiful.

They stand together on the roof looking out on the Tanzanian landscape, absorbing their new surroundings.

Two more foreign students enter, a man and a woman. The man is tall and skinny with dreadlocks and a goatee and a shaggy looking appearance. The girl wears short, carelessly cut hair but has a beautiful face. Together, they represent the liberal youth of Europe. As they approach and say hello, the Americans turn to greet them.

Dash and Belle: Hello.

Kirby and Bob: Oh, Hello.

They shake hands and introduce themselves. The man speaks very low and steady and calm and the woman wears a brilliant smile and talks energetically with a happy tone that affects everyone around her.

Bob: I'm Bob.

Kirby: And I'm Kirby.

Belle: I am Belle.

Dash: Dash.

Belle: Where are you from?

Bob: We're from America, and you?

Dash: Ahhh! We're from France.

Bob: Ahhh! Cool. Well, we were just admiring our new home. Isn't it beautiful?

Belle: Yes, it's very nice. Have you just come?

Kirby: Yes, just today.

Belle: Cool.

Bob: And you?

Belle: Ahh, we've been here…two days now.

Dash: Do you smoke?

Bob: Excuse me?

Dash: Do you smoke? Ganja? I have some.

Bob: Oh…cool, o.k.

Kirby: Yea, o.k.

They take seats on the broken bench and an additional metal chair where Dash begins to roll a joint. The sun is setting behind them, to stage left. It lights the sky on fire before day turns to twilight.

Bob: So, how was your trip?

Belle: It was nice, 10 hours. And yours?

Bob: Very long, about 15 hours. But we made it, so I guess it was fine.

Belle: Yes, of course. [Giggles.]

At that point, two Tanzanian students enter, singing in Kiswahili as they turn the corner and find the foreign students. Salli carries a guitar.

Sam: *Ohhh, mambo vipi?*[20]

Dash and Belle: *Poa. Mambo?*[21]

Ben and Kirby: *Poa.*

Sam and Salli: *Poa.*[22]

Sam: *Unafanya nini?*[23]

Bob and Kirby smile and suggest they don't understand with looks of bewilderment.

Dash: *Ahh, Tuna…Tunavuta kidogo tu.*[24]

Salli: *Unavuta? Poa.*[25]

Dash: *Ndiyo, karibu.*

---

[20] What's up!

[21] Cool! Hi!

[22] Cool!

[23] What are you doing?

[24] Well, ..err.. we're smoking, just a bit.

[25] Smoking? That's cool.

Sam: Ahhh! *Unasema Kiswahili, poa. Asante!*[26]

They take a seat on the roof to form a circle.

Sam: *Sasa, unaitwa nani?*[27]

Dash: *Ninaitwa*[28] Dash.

Belle: *Na ninaitwa* Belle.

Bob: *uhh…ni-na-itawa* Bob.

Kirby: *na…ni-na-it-i-wa* Kirby.

Sam: Kerby.

Kirby: Kirby.

Sam: Kaerby.

Kirby: Kirby.

Salli: Kirby.

Kirby: Yes! Kirby. And you?

Sam: I am Sam.

Salli: I am Salli.

Kirby: Nice to meet you.

Salli: *Na wewe pia.* Where are you from?

Belle: We are from France. [*Pointing to herself and Dash.*]

Kirby: And we are from America. [*Pointing to herself and Bob.*]

Bob: And you?

Salli: [*Laughing.*] *Tunatoka*[29] Tanzania!

Bob: Ahh, Tanzania.

Sam: *Ndiyo, sisi ni wabonga.*

---

[26] You speak good Kiswahili. Thank you.

[27] So, what's your name?

[28] I'm (called) …

[29] We're from …

Bob: *Wabongo?*

Sam: *Wabongo, ndiyo.* It means Tanzanians.

Bob: Ahh.

Sam: Yes, its slang. We like to use slang like *mambo* and *poa*.

Bob: Ahh, *poa*.

All: *Laugh*

Salli: So, *karibu sana*[30] Tanzania.

Belle and Dash: *Asante.*

Bob and Kirby: *Asante.* So far so good.

Salli: Yes, you will like it here. We have beaches and mountains and rainforests and *simba* and *tembo*.[31] Ohhh, there's so much, I think you will like it very much.

Bob: *Poa.*

Dash has finished rolling the joint. It's a big one. He begins to smoke it and pass it around. Salli begins to play a song on the guitar.

Salli: Zamani zamani zamani sana
Zamani zamani zamani sana
Zamani zamani zamani sana
Zamani zamani zamani sana
Zamani sana, tulikua pamoja
Tuliishi kwa amani bila kuwa na matata
Sasa hatuko pamoja
Tunaishi kwenye vita, tuna shida nyingi
Long long long long time ago
Long long long long time ago
Long long long long time ago
Long long long long time ago
A long time ago, we were together
We lived in peace, we had no worries

---

[30] you're most welcome.

[31] lion and elephant

> Now we are not together
> We live with war, we have many problems.

Bob: I like that, it's very nice. Did you write it?

Salli: Yes, this is my song.

Bob: Cool. I like it. Will you teach it to me someday?

Salli: Yes, I can.

Bob: *Poa.*

Dash: Yes, it's very nice, but maybe we'll add the verse in French?

Salli: *Poa!*

They continue to smoke and play music as the lights fade into night and they all slowly turn in.

A few weeks later, in the afternoon, two new students have joined them: Shuji a Japanese exchange student and another American, Ralph. In all it's Bob, Belle, Dash, Sam, Salli, Shuji, and Ralph.

Shuji: Once again the Americans have surrounded us, man.

Bob: That's right! America doesn't screw around, Shuji.

Shuji: Yes, I know, man. The next thing you're going to do is drop bombs on us all.

Bob: Hey, only if you surprise attack us first.

Shuji: Yea, but that was a military base, man. You guys dropped atomic bombs on two civilian cities.

Bob: Yea, I know. You're right Shuji. That was definitely wrong.

Ralph: Definitely.

Shuji: Aw, it's o.k., Ralph. I know it wasn't your fault.

Bob: Shuji, you're awesome. Shujination!

Shuji: Shujination!

All: [Laugh.]

Sam: Aw, but really I think America is a good place to be, right? Much more than here.

Ralph: No, I don't think so. I think it's much better here. I think I would much rather be here.

Sam: *Hapana! Kwa nini?* Surely, you have much more in America. I think to live in America it would be very nice.

Ralph: Yes, it is nice because we have many things, but for me these things don't matter. In America, we have fancy cars and big houses, but all this doesn't matter. I like it much better here.

Sam: But why? We have nothing here. We are a poor country.

Ralph: Yes, economically, you are poor. I don't think anyone will deny that. But you have something here that most Americans can't appreciate. Here, even though you don't have expensive material possessions, you have a respect for life and a sense of existence that is rarely found in America.

Sam: I don't know.

Ralph: It's just like "Death of a Salesman". Have you read this play? It's very good. It's by an American who saw the flaws in capitalism. Here, in Tanzania, people appreciate life. People appreciate family and friends and they enjoy their simple life. They don't have fancy things that people in America want so bad. People in America feel like they're not living if they don't have these fancy things. They only care about being successful and making money without regard to inherent human principles. They spend their whole lives working hard to obtain a fortune they couldn't possibly spend in one lifetime. Meanwhile, they've neglected their friends and family and forgotten what life is all about. But here, although most people are poor and live in small, humble houses, I've never seen people more genuinely happy. Just happy to be alive with their family and friends, that's it.

Sam: This seems very crazy to me. To me, I know America is a great place with many opportunities.

Bob: Well, here I think you're right, Sam. America is a great place for opportunities. You can find a job, work your way up, and provide for your family. This is a good thing about America.

At this point, Bob's phone rings and he picks it up and continues to talk in the background as the discussion continues.

Bob: Hello.

Ralph: Yes, my grandfather used to tell me stories of when his family came from Poland and he would stand on the street corners of Baltimore, selling flyers for a penny a piece…

Bob: What? What is it?

Ralph: …From there, he sent his kids to school and this has brought me here, halfway across the world, a place my grandfather never would have dreamed of me being.

Bob: Really…

Sam: Well, I think I would like it very much then.

Ralph: *Karibu sana.* Anytime.

Sam: *Poa.*

Bob: What?! Oh, man! That's horrible! When was this? …O.K. Thanks for telling me. See ya.

Shuji: What's going on, man? Was that Kirby? Where's she been lately?

Bob: No, that wasn't Kirby. There's been a shooting at an American university; more than twenty people have been killed.

All: [Gasp.]

Ralph: Again? You gotta be kidding me?

Bob: Yea, some crazy guy stood on top of the football stadium and shot a bunch of people.

Belle: Oh, my gosh.

Ralph: It's not that strange. I think I'm starting to get used to it.

Dash: Ahh, the crazy Americas with their guns. Always shooting this and that. What is it with these guns?

Bob: I don't know. I really don't get it. I don't know who these people are. You see, this is what I'm talking about. This would never happen in Tanzania, never. But in America this shit happens repeatedly. It makes it shitty to be American. To come from a place where people can buy guns and go to war before they can get a beer and relax. That's shitty.

Belle: Yes, this is bad.

Ralph: Very bad.

Just then, a noise begins to grow from the bottom of the hill where the dorm sits. Everyone stands to look. The noise grows to an audible shouting of men. They are chanting in Kiswahili. Then, beeping of car horns, randomly and loud. A few more moments and the shatter of a window followed by the screams of women. It all blends in a sound of chaos. People begin to run up the hill.

Shuji: Oh, man. What's going on?

Bob: I don't know. Should we go see?

Sam: No, I don't think so. This can be very dangerous. I think some of the students have protested.

Ralph: About what? What's going on?

Salli: It's about money. It's always about money.

Bob: This sounds very bad. I think we should go down and make sure everything's all right. [*He begins to leave.*]

Sam: No, Bob. I don't think you should.

But Bob has already left. Those remaining watch over the side of the roof. The sound of chaos continues. They all watch for a few moments before they see Bob running back up the hill.

Sam: Oh, no. Here he comes. He's bleeding.

Sam and Salli go down to meet him. A few moments later they return to the roof. Bob is holding a bloody rag over his nose.

Belle: Oh, Bob. Are you o.k.? [*She runs to him and begins to care for him.*]

Bob: It's just my nose. I was hit with a stick when I went down there. It's o.k., the bleeding will stop.

Salli: I don't know. I think you should go to the infirmary.

Bob: I'm not going down there again. You're nuts. I feel safe and sound here on this roof.

Dash: So, what happened? What's going on down there?

Bob: It's crazy, man. The students are very angry. They are going crazy. They're attacking the *daladalas*[32], rocking them back and forth and hitting people with sticks. Some people were in a *daladala* and other people were trying to get on, but the students with sticks were attacking them. I guess they didn't want anybody to leave. It was crazy. Then they saw me trying to help so they hit me. Eventually everyone got out.

Sam: Oh my! This is very bad. I'm very sorry for you. I don't know who these people are. This should not be happening. I don't know about this protest.

Ralph: Protest! This isn't a protest, this is a riot.

Then, Sam gets a call and Salli shortly after. End of scene.

One week later, Bob and Shuji are up on the roof. It's night again.

---

[32] minivans used for local bus service

Bob: This sucks, Shuji. This place is dead.

Shuji: I know, man. Everybody's gone.

Bob: I can't believe they kicked everyone out. It doesn't seem right.

Shuji: I don't know, man, it was pretty crazy down there. You got hit in the face with a stick, man.

Bob: Yea, but they didn't have to kick everyone out. Sam and Salli didn't do anything, they were right here with us. It was just a bunch of hooligans on a power trip.

Shuji: What do you mean?

Bob: It was just some kids from the Student Union who wanted to stand up for their fellow students. So they hit them with sticks and scare the shit out of them. That's not a good way to demonstrate your frustrations. It just pisses people off. It pisses me off. Now all of our friends have had to leave and they're denied their education because of these kids.

Shuji: Yea. This sucks, man.

Bob: Damn right it sucks. I wish I could do something. I wish we had some sort of voice. I don't think anyone will listen to us.

Shuji: Hey, where's Kirby been lately? I haven't seen her.

Bob: Neither have I. She's got a new boyfriend.

Shuji: Really, Tanzanian?

Bob: No, he's American, which is weird. Why do you come halfway across the world to find a friend from your own country? From your own town? He's from our town.

Shuji: Yea, I don't know. So what about you and Belle?

Bob: What about us? There is no us?

Shuji: Yea, but there should be, I think.

Bob: Really? Why?

Shuji: You don't like her?

Bob: Yea, of course I do. She's cool.

Shuji: So, she likes you and you like her. What's the problem?

Bob: Wait, she likes me? How do you know?

Shuji: Oh, come on, man. It's obvious. She definitely likes you.

Bob: Really? What is that – some sort of Japanese fortune telling trick?

Shuji: [*Sarcastically.*] Yes, of course. I saw it written in the stars.

Bob: Really?

Shuji: Noooooo, she told me.

Bob: Oh, cool.

Then, Salli and Sam enter wearing bright smiles and singing as usual. Bob and Shuji jump up to greet them.

Bob: Hey! They're back. *Mambo vipi?*

Sam and Salli: *Poa!*

Shuji: Hey, what are you guys doing here? We were just talking about how much we missed you.

Salli: Well, we just got back from the administrator's offices…

Bob: And?

Salli: And, we talked to them about our involvement in the strike. That we weren't responsible in any way. That we shouldn't be penalized for the irresponsibility of others.

Bob: And?

Sam: And they said o.k.!

Shuji: O.K. what?

Salli: O.K., we're pardoned. We won't be punished for the strike. They've already identified the students involved in leading the strike and they're taking action now.

Sam: We can move back in this weekend.

Bob: No way. Awesome.

Sam: Yes, *Poa!* So, we've called everyone to the roof to celebrate with us.

People begin to enter the roof and mingle with the others.

Salli: Long long long long time ago

Long long long long time ago

Ralph: Wait, Salli. Don't sing that one.

Salli: *Hamna shida.*[33] I modified it a bit:

Long long long long time ago
Long long long long time ago
A long time ago, we weren't together
We had worries, we had no peace
Now we are together
We live without war, we have no problems

Ralph: *Poa.*

Bob: I'd like to propose a toast! Excuse me, everyone. Thank you. So, when I came to the University of Dar es Salaam, I was not expecting most of the things that have happened to happen. But they did.

Ralph: Duh!

All: *[Laugh.]*

Bob: Yea, sorry. I did not expect to meet all of you wonderful friends and I did not expect to get hit in the face with a stick.

All: *[Laugh.]*

Bob: Thanks. I did not expect to meet a beautiful girl from

---

[33] No problem, no worries.

France, who I can barely understand, but love dearly. I did not expect my friend to wander off with another American who she loves dearly.

Kirby: Not!

Kirby's Boyfriend: Hey!

All: [*Laugh.*]

Bob: I did not expect my friends to be expelled and thrown off campus. I did not expect to be alone again in my dorm so soon. But then, the incredible happened. Sam and Salli used their voice and fought for their rights. I did not expect this. Now, we are on the roof having a great time and one week ago I certainly did not expect this. So, I'd like to propose a toast to Sam and Salli. Thanks for using your voice. Thanks for giving us a reason to celebrate. *Hongera!* [34]

All: [*Laugh.*] *Hongera!*

Belle: Did you really mean all that, *monsieur* Bob?

Bob: *Oui, madame* Belle[35].

Belle: Even the part about the French girl?

Bob: Yes, *madame*. Even the part about the French Girl.

---

[34] Congratulations.

[35] Yes, Mrs. Belle (Beautiful).

"Judges on Trial"

by Frowin Paul Nyoni

Characters:

Judge Noma

Panajambo

Clerk

The Ghost Judge

Ghosts

Ghost I

Ghost II

Ghost III

Setting:

Courtroom in the fictional country of *Panajambo.*

Court room. The court is fully packed with the audience. Soft music plays in the background as the Court Clerk enters with a large pile of files and goes to sit at his desk. A big wall clock strikes nine. The clerk straightens up, looks at the audience and shouts above the music.

Clerk: Cooooooooort!

The Music stops. Enters Judge Noma, ceremoniously. The judge sits.

Clerk: *[Alarmed and angry.]* This is ridiculous. I was told there would be three judges. Where are the others?

Judge Noma: Stop being silly, call in the accused.

Clerk: But your honour....

Judge: Call in the accused or I will also leave the courtroom.

Clerk: I'm sorry, your honour, but it is my duty to know...

Judge Noma: It is also my duty to judge this case, but ooooh. *[He storms out.]*

Clerk: Oooh no, Judge please! *[He follows out.]*

Judge Noma: *[Enters, followed by the clerk.]* I feel better now. But you must hurry up before my stomach disturbs me again.

Clerk: Yes, your honour, but what happened to the other judges?

Judge: I will tell you. They are dead.

Clerk: Dead, from what? I don't believe this!

Judge: They were eaten by the moo..., mooo...nster, monster. *[Runs around the court, followed by the clerk.]*

Clerk: *[Hesitantly.]* Where is it, your honour? There is no monster here.

Judge: Call in the accused or else I will be eaten before I finish presiding over this case.

Clerk: Eeh ... bring in the accused!

Enters Panajambo, the accused. He looks very thin and frail. He is crawling since he is too weak to walk. He is holding a police crown hat in one of his hands. He goes to stand at the accused box.

Clerk: Where is the police officer who was supposed to escort you in?

Panajambo: It is a sad story sir. He has been eaten by the monster. Only this is left. *[Shows the hat.]*

Judge Noma: Where?

Panajambo: Just outside the door, your honour!

Judge: Where! *[He falls from his seat and the clerk runs and helps him to sit again. The judge is trembling furiously.]*

Clerk: Your honour, *[in a low tone]* the court is fully packed: do not behave foolishly.

Judge Noma: *[Angrily.]* What? Is being scared of death acting foolish? Wait until the monster comes after you, then your senses will begin working properly. Stupid bastard! *[Looks at him for a minute.]* What are the charges?

Clerk: Your honour, before I submit this case to you, may you please introduce yourself, mention your credentials, and tell the court why you consider yourself the most competent to judge this case.

Judge Noma: *[Smiling.]* That is easy. I'm the only...

The side door is opened and enters Ghost Judge. Judge Noma ducks under the table. Ghost Judge flushes Judge Noma from under the table and sits him in his chair.

Ghost Judge: My dear friend, you cannot preside over this case. Who you are to judge this man?

Judge Noma: I'm Judge Noma, the most honourable supreme court just ...

Ghost Judge: Stop that nonsense. I know who you are. We were together before the monster caught and killed me.

I remember when Panajambo first cried for help; you were busy chairing conferences on development aid, environment and development, workshops on sustainable utilisation of natural resources, seminars on poverty alleviation and others on integrated rural development, participatory rural research, development from below, and community-based participatory planning. Remember the annual concerts, dinners, and charity walks to raise money to fund a hundred and one projects to develop Panajambo and his folks?

Judge Noma: What is wrong with that? Panajambo and his fellows needed all those things.

Ghost Judge: True: they needed them and we provided them. But, did you make follow-up to ensure that our taxpayers' money was used properly by Panajambo and his folks?

Clerk: [Addressing Ghost Judge.] Your honour, can you be seated so that we continue with this case.

Ghost Judge: There is no case here. I'm off. [Walks towards the door and stops.] Goodbye, honourable justice. See you soon in hell. [Exits.]

Clerk: Your honour, may we continue please!

Judge Noma: [Recollecting.] Yes, continue!

Clerk: Remember the court asked for your credentials and people here still want to hear them.

Judge Noma: I hold a Diploma in legal affairs, an Advanced Diploma in paralegal affairs, a Bachelor's degree in jurisprudence, a Postgraduate Diploma in the law of tort, a Masters degree in constitutional and labour law, a Doctorate in the law of contract and tax law, and a Post Doctoral advanced diploma in family law. [Pauses.] Do you want me to continue?

Clerk: No, it is more than enough, your honour. Thanks very much, your honour. Let me now present before you the accused Panajambo bin Panajambo, who is alleged to have committed the greatest of the greatest crimes of all times. He is a witch, more devilish and satanic than the Wizard of OZ. When the monster was first seen in his village, he tamed it, nurtured it, and gave it food and shelter. When it began eating his children, relatives, and neighbours, he did nothing to stop it. The monster went on a rampage and he did nothing to stop it. The monster ate all his folk. It invaded the neighbouring villages and wiped them out. It then crossed rivers and oceans and came here where our folks are mowed down like locusts when sprayed with DDT. So, we went after him, and brought him to this court.

Judge Noma: I'm sort of confused...should we just sit here and continue with this case or go out and hunt down the monster?

Clerk: Your honour, the bird in you hands is worth ten times more than ten birds out there in a tree. Let us prosecute this man quickly and run away before the monster catches us!

Ghost Judge: *[Enters laughing.]* Haaa, haa! Hey, there is no way you can run away from the monster. It has got many faces, many colours; it's visible and sometimes invisible. It can be here in court, up here dressed up as a judge!

Judge Noma: Do you want to say I'm the monster? I will charge you for contempt of court!

Ghost Judge: Go ahead and charge a ghost! This is ridiculous! Are all human beings as stupid as him? May be today, but during our time, we were not. Even Judge Noma was not stupid. He was a wonderful judge who, from a mere clerk, shot up the rank and file to be the honourable justice of the Supreme Court. The super genius who studied law privately and passed all exams with distinctions. We all admired and respected him. He chaired every meeting and ....

Judge Noma: Hey! Stop day dreaming in my court. Can you please go out, I have important cases to preside over and I don't have much time.

Ghost Judge: *[Goes to the accused.]* Goodbye and good luck, Panajambo. But never expect any Justice from Judge Noma *[pointing at Judge Noma]*. He thinks he has invented law, and law to him states "whoever steps into the accused box is guilty." I will soon see you all. *[Exits.]*

Clerk: My apologies for any distractions. Let us now proceed.

Ghost Judge: *[Standing by the door.]* Proceed doing what? There is no case here, and if there is one, then Judge Noma is not the right person to preside over it. Unfortunately he is the only judge alive.

Clerk: Are you telling us that Judge Noma is not the right person? Why?

Judge Noma: Clerk, let us proceed with the case. Stop wasting your time talking to a ghost.

Ghost Judge: You will soon join us, your honour. Bye. *[Exits.]*

Judge Noma: Now the accused, what do you plead?

Panajambo: Before I plead anything, your honour, may I please say something?

Judge Noma: Say it quickly.

Panajambo: Paukwa.

Judge and Clerk: Pakawa.

Enter ghost actors and actresses, and each say a section of the following verse.

> paliondokea Chanjagaa
>
> kajenga nyumba kakaa
>
> Mwanangu mwana Siti
>
> Kijino kama chikichi

Cha kujengea vikuta

na milango ya kupita

Naam twaibu [36]

The ghosts play the drums and dance.

Panajambo: [*Narrating.*] Long, long ago, in the land of Mtazameni, I and my people lived happily and peacefully.

The ghosts sing the following song.

selemani nipasulie mbao

aliya kweche kweche,

aliya kweche msumeno.[37]

The song is sung while ghost-performers dance to portray various occupations. After a while they exit.

Panajambo: But one day a strange creature was seen in our village.

The ghosts enter the stage, singing the following song.

Kalunde pepepee kalunde peepepee! ×3. [38]

Panajambo: As we were sitting around a fire place, eating roasted maize and narrating stories, a man rushed in and shouted that he had seen a monster and he described it as a creature that is as tall as a coconut tree; another came in and said it was as long as a snake; another said it was thunder; and, yet another said it was huge like

---

[36] Once upon a time there was a man called Chanjagaa / Who built a house and stayed in it / My daughter Siti has a tooth like a palm tree / That is used to build walls and doors / Yes, your honour!

[37] Saw wood for me / The seesaw cries kweche kweche / As you saw the wood

[38] Kalunde is coming, Kalunde is coming. (Translated from the Kiha)

a baobab tree; another that it was tall like a mountain. We were confused. But as we were wondering what to do, the monster began killing people.

The ghosts sing the following song.

> sote tunalia, sote tunalia.[39]

The ghosts then explain how they were caught by the monster.

Ghost 1: The monster caught me after I had raped fifty women.

Ghost 2: The monster caught me because I was a sugar-mammy: I loved sex more than food. I used to do it with one in the morning, another at ten, yet another one at twelve, two in the evening, and four at night.

Ghost 3: The monster caught me because I used to commit adultery.

Ghost 4: The monster caught me after I had sex with a witch doctor in search of a baby.

Ghost 5: The monster caught me because I used to work in a bar, and every night I had sex with different men.

Ghost 1: The monster caught me because I was too poor to afford a pair of shoes, so I walked barefoot.

Ghost 2: The monster caught me after my father was conned by crop buyers and I was forced into prostitution to support our family.

Ghost 3: The monster caught me because, as a lorry driver, I was stupid enough to have casual sex with different women without protection at every substation where I stopped.

The ghosts sing the following song.

> Sote tunalia eh sote tunalia

---

[39] We are all crying, we are all crying.

Panajambo: We gathered and laid strategies. We gathered all the weapons we could find and went after the monster.

The ghosts continue singing.

> *Tuende pamozi nu mtima umo ×2*
> *jamani twende,*
> *twende pamozi tuende pamozi nu mtima umo.*[40]

Panjambo: People continued to die. We realised that some of us walked barefoot, and the monster pierced and poisoned their legs. So we ordered shoes for everyone. But People continued to die. As some put the right shoe on the left foot and the left shoe on the right foot, and hence could not run fast and the monster caught them. Some didn't put on their shoes at all. They left them at home, where they treasured them as souvenirs and walked barefoot. People continued to die.

The ghosts sing the following song.

> *Mama mdogo njoo nione nimekatika kidole.* [41]

Panjambo: Lamentations, cries of agony, wailing cries filled our sky. The monster hit every home. But people were scared of disclosing the source of death. They attributed the deaths to 'long illnesses', 'chest related diseases', 'High blood pressure', 'low blood pressure', 'breathing problems', 'severe headaches', 'heart diseases', and so on. So lies and cries filled our air. Everybody lied: family members and friends, doctors, witch doctors, religious leaders, village elders and neighbours. I remember telling them not to lie and to call a spade a spade. "It is the monster who is killing you, put on shoes when walking and never fight the monster unprotected," I shouted. No one would listen to me, and those who listened called me a traitor.

---

[40] Lets all go together with one heart / Lets go / Lets all go together with one heart. (Translated from the Kinyanja)

[41] Mother (mother's young sister) come to see me as I have lost a toe!

They blocked me from caring for the victims and attending funerals, and they accused me of bringing a bad omen.

The ghosts sing the following song and exit.

Ai ndege ndege ai ndegeilahinda ×2

Ai ndege itagila maso nyamalila lila genda. [42]

Panjambo: The monster continued killing people. Our village was wiped out; our near and distant villages were wiped out. Then the monster crossed the river and went to the land of Judge Noma. I was the only survivor. The monster was scared of me. I never walked barefoot, I always carried protected shields. One day when I was resting under a tree, soldiers from the land of Judge Noma arrested me and brought me to this court, and here I am, your honour.

Judge Noma: Who are these people who came in to dramatise? I thought that you are the only one left?

Panajambo: These were ghost-relatives of mine were killed by the monster long time ago!

Judge Noma: Mmmh! But, if you were not affected by the monster, why are you so weak, and why do you look like you are dying?

Panajambo: I am suffering from diabetes, renal insufficiency, pulmonary oedema, retinopathy, hepatilopathy, gout, heparesis, malaria, typhoid, dysentery, anaemia, malnutrition...

Judge Noma: Okay! Okay! Stop it!

Panajambo: I haven't finished yet, your honour.

Elephantiasis, lep...

---

[42] The aeroplane is moving / The aeroplane has no eyes but it moves. (Translated from the Kiha)

Judge Noma: *[Bangs the table.]* Stop it! Now, what do you plead?

Panajambo: I can't say it, your honour.

Judge Noma: Say it. Otherwise I will charge you for contempt of court.

Panajambo: You are guilty.

Judge Noma: Who, me?

Panajambo: Yes, you and the other judges.

Judge Noma: But the others are dead!

Panajambo: All the same. It doesn't change the verdict.

Judge Noma: Wait a minute: What are my charges?

Panajambo: When we cried for your help, you heard us, but did nothing to help us fight the monster.

Judge Noma: You chicken head, have you forgotten that we gave you millions of millions of our taxpayers' money to help you fight the monster?

Panajambo: Sorry, your honour: I swear to the gods that I didn't see even a cent of your money.

Ghosts enter the stage one by one saying:

Ghost I: I got the money and I used it to establish the so called international schools, English-medium: four secondary schools, two primary schools, six high schools, and ten nursery schools

Ghost II: I got the money and I used it to buy twenty-five *daladalas* and to build four tourist hotels!

Ghost III: I got the money and I opened a Swiss bank account!

Ghost IV: I got the money and with my briefcase NGO, I spent it visiting beauty spots inside and outside the country.

Panajambo: You see, no money reached or benefited me and

114

my people in the poor urban and rural areas, and we were the people targeted to benefit.

Judge Noma: That is not my fault.

Panajambo: It is your fault, as you didn't make follow-up to ensure that the money was spent appropriately.

Judge Noma: So, what can I do?

Ghost I: Nothing at the moment.

Ghost II: It is already too late.

Ghost III: We will take you to the other world ourselves.

Ghosts I: We can't wait for the monster to deal with you.

The ghosts grab Judge Noma and take him out. They come back and sit on judges' chairs.

Ghost I: Clerk, wake up the accused.

Clerk: [*Goes to the accused. Examines him and shakes his head.*] He can never wake up, your honour.

Ghosts I, II, and III: What do you mean?

Clerk: His heart has stopped pumping.

Ghosts I, II, and III: What do you mean?

Clerk: He is cold.

Ghosts I, II, and III: What do you mean? Is he dead?

Clerk: I am not sure, but he is not moving.

1st Ghost: [*Advances towards Panajambo.*] He can't be dea....

All Ghosts: [*Singing*]
   Only ghosts will remain
   Only ghosts will remain
   To swim in the rivers and oceans
   And drink the protected waters of the Nile
   Thames, Rhine, Ganges, Yangtze-kiang
   And the Amazon

Only ghosts will remain
Only ghosts will remain
To swim in the rivers and oceans
To dwell in the empty cities and towns
To sit in the classrooms
And enjoy remote learning
Through the internet.

Others join in the singing. Panajambo slowly wakes up and joins in the singing. Enters Judge Noma. All stop singing and look at him.

Judge Noma: Let us not lose hope. Something can be done.

All: Something can be done?

Judge Noma: *[Turning to the audience]* Yes, but what should be done?

"The Route to Success"

by Yunus Ng'umbi

Characters:

Kigwanda, young man

Father

Mother

Msakatani, friend

Lukungu, sister

Uncle

Witchdoctor

Head of the Family

Family Members

Mswande, neighbour to family

Sipyusi, neighbor to Msakatani

Setting:

Tanzania

Scene 1

The curtain opens. Mother and seven children are seen sitting down and listening to the father tell stories. One of the elder sons by the name of Kigwanda is also there.

Father: ....Ants are very tiny insects; they are very co-operative. Once they decide to do something, everyone feels responsible. They can build their own house within a very short period of time. Hard work and cooperation to them is essential for success. Similarly, in our times, I used to read the book titled Animal Farm by George Orwell. Animals succeeded to get rid of human control through revolution. The revolution was possible through cooperation. Pigeons, geese, cats, sheep, snowballs, and others felt like one... Success comes through hard work and cooperation.

[*Coughs*] My children, telling you stories does not mean I'm satisfied with this life. Every turn I make, I meet with children asking for money to buy clothes, food, fees, and so forth. I don't know when I'm going to get rid of this problem. Kigwanda, you deserve to have your own house now at least to serve your young brothers and sisters and your parents as well. You are old enough to start your family. I think the money you get as a monthly salary from the Tea Company can help you.

Kigwanda: [*After being quiet*] I'm planning to terminate my employment and start a business; I think it pays. I'll join my fellow boys to sell some fruit first and, if I succeed, I'll go on with other things. Thereafter I'll take care of you all.

Mother: [*In trembling voice*] All through the night I have been dreaming about two boys fighting to get a certain lady. All of a sudden, one was killed. The death of the boy meant that the killer was jailed; thus, both failed in their mission to have the lady. [*Slowly standing to go out, she falls down in attempt to pull behind her three-legged chair.*] Osh!.... old is no longer gold. I'm now a child.

[*Lukungu rushes to support her and they go out.*]

Father: [*After a moment*] Your mother is old. She thinks a lot about her children. You need to let her also get a rest.

Kigwanda: ......All that you are saying is our duty to put into practice. It is high time for me and my young brothers and sisters to take care of our parents.... Mmmm...next week after getting my salary, I'll go to collect some fruit at Ifyasolo and start selling them.

Father: It's a good decision. I don't have any objection. Ask your ancestors to be with you in all your doings.

[*Father exits the stage.*]

Scene 2

Kigwanda is standing stage right, on a street corner, with Msakatani's house on stage left.

Kigwanda [*Monologue, standing on a street*] I hear that Msakatani is living a very luxurious life in town. Where he got the money nobody knows. Probably because he appropriated all the money he got after selling his deceased brother's house.

[*Msakatani enters.*]

Kigwanda: Ooh, my best friend! I think I'm not mistaken that you're Mr. Msakatani. Are you?

Msakatani: [*Touching his neck tie*] Why ask such a silly question? We were grazing cattle together in our childhood. I was one of your best friends. What makes you hesitate even in remembering my name? [*Puts his briefcase down.*]

Kigwanda: [*While putting his plastic bag down*] The way you are. You do not seem to be the same person I used to see before. You have changed a lot!

Msakatani: Changed a lot? I'm trying to nurture my future life through business. I'm now a man with growing businesses and I own two big shops, a house, and three cars.

Kigwanda: Great! I envy the way you appear. Your success is mine too.

Msakatani: Mine is mine and yours is yours. Tell me to give you some advice on how to achieve your success. What I have belongs to my family, not yours. Let us go together up to where I live.

Kigwanda: The sun will shine only on the one who stands first. Since you left home, I've been working at the Tea Company with the aim of escaping poverty. But what I have achieved is just the opposite.

Msakatani: You are too wordy! Mere words cannot help you attain anything. Let us speak in the language which results in wealth. [*They reach Msakatani's compound.*] This is my compound. These two shops, cars, and the house are all mine. I'm planning to build another big house for renting.

Kigwanda: In fact I'm satisfied with what you have. Again I beg your help. What did you do to reach this stage? I want to be the same as you.

Msakatani: [*Laughs*] You need to be very courageous and tolerant as well. If you can manage these, life will be very simple. I'm ready to offer you a house near the next street where you can start your business. If you are ready, I can send you somewhere with a little money, but with the guarantee of a high profit in return.

Kigwanda: [Nodding his head as a sign of agreement] I'm ready for everything provided that it won't ruin my life.

Msakatani: Tomorrow, early in the morning, I'll send you somewhere. It is the very place I went to gain wealth.

Kigwanda: [Draws the image of the wealthiest person] If I could be the sun maker....

Msakatani: What would you do?

Kigwanda: I would push it to hurry up so that tomorrow comes early to fulfill my ambitions. By the way, how will we go?

Msakatani: On foot. We'll start our journey early in the morning, at the first cockcrow.

Scene 3

Early in the morning. Kigwanda and Msakatani walk away from the compound toward the witchdoctor's house.

Kigwanda: I didn't sleep well during the night as I kept on thinking about how I can travel and gain wealth. [Yawning] I don't know where we are going, but because I'm struggling for wealth, I have nothing to fear.

Msakatani: Don't worry. Everything that we are doing is to attain the best life in the future.

[After a long journey.]

Msakatani: We are nearly approaching the targeted house [Pointing with his finger], that house beside the eucalyptus tree.

Kigwanda: Oooh! What am I going to say?

Msakatani: Tell him all that you want and you have to agree with what the doctor advises you to do. If you don't agree, your dream won't be successful.... This is the very house. Do you see the queue of people? Go and queue for service.

I'll be back soon because I can't tolerate staying here. Be attentive because the doctor may call anyone by name and tell him to come in for assistance.

Kigwanda: [Holding his little plastic bag] Does he know my name?

Msakatani: He knows the names of all people in this world and yours too.

[Msakatani exits the stage.]

Kigwanda: [Monologue] I'm now alone; no one is likely to converse with me as they are all seriously waiting for assistance.

Witchdoctor: [Comes out from the service room.] It's time to stop offering service today. Those remaining have to wait until tomorrow morning. I have several rooms for my clients. You'll sleep here!

[Msakatani enters.]

Kigwanda: The time for offering service is over. That is why you see me sitting here desperately. I and other customers won't be attended to today. We have to wait until tomorrow morning.

Msakatani: Worry not! You need to be patient if at all you want to succeed.

Kigwanda: [Taking the boiled sweet-potatoes from his plastic bag] Let's have our dinner! [While eating] I'm somehow shocked by some things that I happened to see in the witchdoctor's service room.

Msakatani: [Joking] What were you looking for? That's the witchdoctor's room where the world is looked at in different ways from what you know. All that you saw is helpful in serving peoples' lives.

Kigwanda: I'm a man; anything to fear is fear itself. Why should I fear minor things like these? (*He bends down to think on what will happen to him*).

Msakatani: Now, it's getting dark and I'm told that during the night no one is allowed to walk out. It's the time for angels to perform their duties.

[*Darkness*]

[*The next morning*]

Msakatani: Wake up to get prepared for the session. It's the second cockcrow. Be careful…. Remember what I told you. Whatever the witchdoctor asks you regarding what are you able to do, say you are ready for everything provided that it can't ruin your life.

Kigwanda: I'll do so brother!

Msakatani: Be careful with the doctor's style of calling people in. I forgot to tell you yesterday: when you are called, take off your shoes before entering the room.

Kigwanda: I'll do as you say.

[*After a long stay, Kigwanda hears a certain sound.*]

Voice: Haaaa!!! The next creature must come in to explain his problems.

[*Kigwanda enters the room.*]

Voice from the Calabash: Tell us, what brought you here?

Kigwanda: [*Trembling*] Vatwa.[43] It's nothing more than requesting wealth.

Voice from the Calabash: Wealth? What do you want to own?

---

[43] To mean kings

Kigwanda: Beautiful cars, a big house and a big shop–only these!

Voice from the Calabash: *[A sign of laugh]* Ha! Ha! Ha! All these are possible and a number of people have been coming to ask for the same and now are very successful. How much do you have in your pocket to start your business?

Kigwanda: Thirty thousand shillings.

Voice from the Calabash: Put them down. *[The witchdoctor collects the money and puts it in a calabash.]*

Witchdoctor: You need to abide by certain conditions. This amount of money should only be used for buying commodities for sale at the point of starting your business. Don't use this money for anything else. Don't give any amount of money to anyone on Wednesdays. On other days, you're allowed to do so. *[He continues, holding bead like objects]* These objects have to be burnt once every month. Burn them in the fire until they give smoke. You've to pay fifty thousand shillings for the service.

Kigwanda: Ok. All these are minor things. I'll do as you say. Are there other conditions?

Witchdoctor: No, but every month you need to come and tell us the progress of your business.

Kigwanda: Ok. Thank you!

[He goes out.] Brother! I'm finished; we may start our journey back home.

Msakatani: As a starting point, and as I promised you, I give you a house to open your shop. This house was formerly owned by one of my best friends, but he is no longer alive. Later on you can find your own place where you can proceed with your business.

Kigwanda: *(Smiling)* Thank you brother! Tomorrow I'll go to Magida to collect some commodities with my thirty thousand shillings.

Scene 4

After two days. The shop is on stage right and the village is on stage left.

Kigwanda: [*Nodding his head to signify agreement*] This is what I want! Clothes are very marketable nowadays! Tomorrow I'll add other things to speed up my business.

[*After everything is sold*] Nothing is impossible under the sun. I'll adhere to all the conditions given by the doctor. Let me take the pot and the bead-like objects ready to burn as instructed by the doctor.

[*The smoke comes out*] Things will be ok very soon. [*He sneezes.*] Now, it's okay. Let me hide them until next month.

[*Enters Mswande.*]

Mswande: *Sa filo.* [*Greets*]

Kigwanda: Oooh! I'm fine. Have a chair to sit please! How is home and your neighbors, I mean my family?

Mswande: [*Wipes his nose.*] Aaaaa! They are somehow fine.

Kigwanda: What do you mean by the phrase "somehow"?

Mswande: You are a man and I'm sure that what I'm going to say cannot make you collapse. Your mother has passed away today. I'm told to give you this information and to say that the burial ceremony will be tomorrow.

Kigwanda: [*Sighs.*] Wait a bit so that I can get prepared to leave.

[*Walk across stage to where family is mourning.*]

Kigwanda: *[Monologue.]* My family is highly shocked by the death of our beloved mother. I will suggest that my young sister Lukungu should stay with me so that she can help with my business.

[Father enters.]

Kigwanda: I'm planning to take Lukungu so that she can help me with sales in the shop in my absence. The shop is very full, but I will write down the prices so that she will know what to do.

Father: Ok. You're the only son who seems to have vision in your life and the whole family as well. Take Lukungu and the rest of the family members will be looking for your assistance morally and materially. *[Father exits the stage.]*

Scene 5

One month later in the shop on stage right and then walking to the village, stage left.

Kigwanda: *[Monologue.]* Let me burn my objects so as to speed up my business as usual.

[Few hours later]

Lukungu: Brother! There's someone in the shop asking for you. He says, he is from our village.

Kigwanda: From our village? Don't you know him?

Lukungu: I think I happened to see him one day. It is better that you come and ask him what he wants from you.

Kigwanda: *[Washes his hands after the exercise and goes to his shop to meet the guest]* Good morning!

Guest: *[Stands as a sign of respect]* Good morning sir!

Kigwanda: *[Looking at him carefully]* If I'm not mistaken, I happened to see you on one of the social occasions, but I don't remember, may you remind me who you are?

Guest: *[Smiles]* I knew that you don't know me. I'm the young brother of your sister in-law.

Kigwanda: Oooh! I'm glad to know you. Any news from home?

Guest: No need of hiding: your young brother has died.

Kigwanda: What? What a misfortune! My journey to the witchdoctor….. *[Talking by himself]*. When did he die?

Guest: This morning and the burial ceremony will be this evening.

Kigwanda: *[In a low voice]* Don't tell Lukungu of the death of her brother. *[He calls Lukungu who is outside]* Lukungu, our brother at home is sick and I'm told to go to take him to the hospital and you have to be there to take care of our sister in-law's children in her absence. Now get prepared to leave just now.

Scene 6

Family's home in the village.

Kigwanda: (Monologue). What a misfortune! Within these two months, I have lost three family members: My mother, young brother and my young sister, Lukungu, who died of shock after having heard about the death of her brother. Am I responsible for the death of Lukungu simply because I didn't warn her of our brother's death? We must look for the source; otherwise we'll all die.

(Enters the Head of the Family)

Head of the Family: My fellow family members, I've gathered you here to discuss the deaths in our family. It's not strange to see people dying, but, for us, it is something new. My opinion is that we better find the source of death for our family members.

Kigwanda: *[While sitting on a log near the corner of his father's house]* Now, what do you want us to do?

Head of the Family: I suggest that we consult people with divine power who can tell us the source and how to overcome it.

Father: *[Coughing; after a while]* Up to this age, I have never experienced the abrupt loss of children and wife within a short period like this. We better agree with the head's suggestion.

Head of the Family: Who will go on our behalf? Kigwanda and who else?

Kigwanda: *[Interrupts]* No, I can't. Appoint another person, I suggest.

Father: Kigwanda's young sister and her uncle – I think they are the very persons to go. Agreed?

Members: Yes! *[Kigwanda's sister and uncle are seen nodding their heads in agreement.]*

[Darkness]

[Uncle and Lukungu enter]

Uncle: My dear family members, we have spent two days where you sent us to go for divine power consultation. I and my daughter struggled a bit to get the exact information on who is bewitching our family. We eventually got the answer that the enemy is within our family. *[He continues]* We don't need to end here; rather we should consult the second, the third, and the fourth divine powers to be sure. If they all argue the same, we'll start asking individuals in the family.

Head of the Family: Thank you for your report. I now declare the meeting closed until next week when we'll arrange on where to go for further information about the deaths. See you next week.

Scene 7

After three days. Kigwanda's shop on stage right, with Msakatani's house on stage left, and the witchdoctor's house in the middle, back of the stage.

Kigwanda: [*After opening his shop*] Wuuuuwi!... Wuuuuwi!...I see the image of my mother, young brother, and Lukungu in my shop. They are smiling, sitting on the floor near the counter. Msakatani! Msakatani! [*Rushes to the next village where Msakatani is living*]..... Wuuuuwi!

He meets Sipyusi.

Sipyusi: Are you calling Msakatani, the one who had two shops and cars over there? Aaaah! There's a very long story about him. His prosperity in business was because of magic power. He killed his parents and some of his relatives and now he has gone mad because he violated one of his witchdoctor's conditions.

Kigwanda: [*Fart*] Where is he now? I want to see him.

Sipyusi: I don't know!

Kigwanda: To hell with your narration. I know how I can resolve this situation. [*Monologue*] I'll go to my witchdoctor now: He is the only one who can resolve my conflicts.

[*He reaches the doctor's house.*]

Witchdoctor: My client, welcome, although you have entered my room without permission. What's the matter?

Kigwanda: My doctor: today I'm shocked. I lost my mother last month and this month my young brother and young sister. My problem is that I have seen them alive in my shop while I and the whole family know that we buried them at the village.

Witchdoctor: *[Laughs]* By the way, how is your business?

Kigwanda: It's very fine.

Witchdoctor: If your business is fine, then what's wrong with you? The re-appearance of your deceased relatives is very normal because they are the ones who are making your business prosper.

Kigwanda: *[Stands]* Do you mean that I'm responsible for the deaths of my relatives?

Witchdoctor: That's ....

[A sound heard]...... Kigwanda has committed suicide!

"The Mop"

by Vicensia Shule

Characters:

Mkarara, Researcher

Kuta, Religious Group Leader

Mdeni, Peasants' representative

Nzambi, Head of Nyakibonga

Debra, *Mzungu*[44]

Ndanwa, Civil servant

Murungu, God of harmony

Man 1, Peasant

Man 2, Peasant

Woman, Peasant

Officer, Government official

People, Villagers

Setting:

Contemporary Nyakibonga

---

[44]   Stranger, someone not from Tanzania – Usually a white person from Europe or America.

Scene 1

On the stage there is an old table with three chairs decorated with balloons. On one side of the entrance lies a small piece of red carpet, which seems unfit for the environment. On the other side, an old Tanzanian flag is placed closely hidden by a pile of used banners for water conservation, HIV/AIDS, gender, and democracy campaigns.

Mkarara: *[Sitting at front corner of the stage writing something in a notebook. Mkarara's voice is heard from back stage.]* One day I heard my parents debating for hours about the general cleanliness of the house. Regardless of their personal behavior, everyone was confident about how to improve the cleaning process, especially for the floor on which children prefer, much of their time, to sit and play. It came to my surprise how the mop became the center of attention. The mop! The mop! The mop! Every single sentence was accompanied by the mop...the mop... the mop. Several questions were asked regarding the quality and quantity of the mops needed: Should we buy a new mop? Should we use the old mop? Should we transform our old clothes into a mop? Regardless of all these difficult questions, the fact was the mop was not even asked which color, material, texture, size, or even where it wanted to be hanged! The mop silently lay on the floor trying to dry itself; it remained calm to the end of the hot discussion.

Mkarara: *[To the audience.]* With a boiling heart, the mop cried silently...'If I were of such little importance, why do they keep on washing me whenever they use me?' And this was my major research question...

[Enter Kuta and Mdeni. They walk silently for a while.]

Mdeni: I beg you Kuta... I know all the ancestors listen to you.

Kuta: They do not listen to myopic requests; they select what to listen to and what not.

Mdeni: His Excellency and his visitors need to be entertained.

Kuta: Of course, but for him, being entertained has nothing to do with the ancestors. It is obvious: If you pay well, the *wacheza ngoma*[45] will come. Dancing for traitors, betrayers, and other criminal guests is no longer a ritual as it used to be.

Mdeni: Kuta, why are you speaking so nasty today? Are you drunk? You have to speak as a learned person.

Kuta: Mdeni, I know you think I'm an idiot... But for sure, if you are, I'm not. You think that we don't know Nzambi and the clique are petting us because 'the dirtier the mop, the dirtier the floor'? So they have to clean us, otherwise...

Mdeni: You talk like all other frustrated people of Nyakibonga. You have to show that you are different. You are a respected religious leader. Why are you working with assumptions and weak generalizations?

Kuta: You think I'm stupid? Do you believe that I'm a fool? Watch your mouth!

Mdeni: Please Kuta, we'll discuss this later. Please, please! We have visitors. If we give them a bad impression, they will believe we are uncivilized.

Kuta: Of course, they are not like us. They are uncivilized according to our customs. Look at the way they talk, sleep, eat, dress, and above all, at how they think about us. They tend to think that they know much about us, while they know nothing... Please Mdeni, spare me a minute to air my voice when they arrive.

Mdeni: [*Loudly.*] No. A big no! [*Progressively lowers his voice.*]

---

45 'Traditional' dancers

Next time they will reject our invitation. They are our development partners.

Kuta: No matter what, I'll say, let them go back if they want to be heard instead of listening. They are our partners in deficiency and not in development.

[Kuta is possessed.]

Kuta: I, the greatest child, representing all children of this land, I know you know we know they are bloody thieves. And my relatives and I normally burn thieves to death. Tell them … If they knew that, will they still be ready to come?

Mdeni: Don't say it loudly please. It is against human rights.

Kuta: Human rights… Yes human rights for who? And they are lucky, I say… very lucky. If it were not them who killed our technology with their second hand religions, today we would have turned all of them into bats – they would never know whether they were mammals or birds.

Mdeni: *[Begging.]* His Excellency is coming. I earnestly beg the great daughters of Nyakibonga …we'll discuss this later.

[Enters a delegation of Nzambi and Debra. All members are attentive as it was expected when the delegation enters except Kuta, who continues talking.]

Kuta: Later, yes later. I know your later is five years. They'll come back after five years.

Mdeni: *[Standing still, preparing to deliver a speech.]* Ladies and gentlemen, Nyakibonge Hoyee! It is a great honor to us today that our hononorable guests have arrived. As it is our tradition, we now invite our dancers to welcome our guests and present their entertainment.

Enters a group of lizombe dancers singing and dancing.

    Karibuni wageni wetu
    Mjisikie mko Nyakibonga

Nyakibonga kisiwa cha amani
Majirani wanatuonea gere[46]

Before they finish, Mdeni cuts them short.

Mdeni: *Asanteni sana wacheza ngoma.* [*To the audience.*] Let us give a big clap [*to dancers*]. You can now go, to give room for discussion on important issues for your development. In case we need you, your leader will be consulted. Your Excellency, these are our distinguished members who have responded to your invitation.

Debra: [*Whispering to Nzambi.*] They are really good at wriggling their waists. It's wonderful! They are representing Nyakibonga very well.

Ndanwa holding files, peeps from the back stage as a signal to Nzambi, who cannot see him.

Nzambi: Even the research proves that! Thank you for the compliments. Next time, they will dance *sindimba*, which is even more attractive than *lizombe*. [*Standing.*] I greet you, my people of Nyakibonga!

People: *Sawa sawa.*[47]

Kuta looks at Nzambi uncertainly.

Nzambi: My people of Nyakibonga …I know you are aware that life is not as easy as we promised. From the depths of my heart, I feel your troubles and pains. That is why I have brought this friend of mine whom I met when I was taking lunch abroad. I sold my idea: the pinches of the people of Nyakibonga and she felt that there is potential for investment here in Nyakibonga. [*Mdeni nods as Nzambi speaks.*]

---

[46] "Our visitors, you are welcome/ feel that you're at Nyakibonga / Nyakibonga the island of peace / our neighbors envy us"

[47] Fine, okay

Debra: *Nasalimia ninyi…mambo?* Nyakhibongah oyee! [48]

People: *[Silent and murmuring.]*

Debra: *[Continues.]* Well, *Nimekuja na maji.*[49] I have brought a water project. Actually, as my friend His Excellency Mr. Nzambi has said, we met during lunch at McDavid restaurant, and, as business people, we thought there is a potential for investment here at Nyakhibongah.. *[Nzambi looks puzzled when Debra says they are business people, Kuta smiles.]* Since I haven't been here, I thought water must be a problem. I cried…tears fell onto my eyes as I saw the road to Nyakhibongah. It was really an adventure…a real safari so to say. *[Nzambi and Mdeni cheer.]* When I watch CYN and BYC stations, I'm informed that malaria is a killer disease in Africa, so I have brought mosquito nets with me too.

Kuta: *[Muttering.]* I should tell you, unless you failed your biology class, malaria mosquitoes will never cease to exist here. Even if you bring some kind of AK 47 nets! And regarding what you think is a water problem, I believe you don't know geography. Water has never been a problem unless you've come with your water problem creation project…. *[Mdeni tries to stop him.]* Don't try to stop me from saying what I think…this is what you call democracy, yes democracy.

Mdeni: *[Softly to Nzambi and Debra.]* She has psychological problems. She has lost both of her parents recently of AIDS.

Debra: *[Whispering.]* Let's do an HIV/AIDS project, then. This is a serious problem. You see HIV makes people here crazy.

Enters Ndanwa with a pot and hides it behind Nzambi. He speaks to Mdeni and they all leave the stage.

---

[48] I'm greeting you…how are things?

[49] I have brought water.

Nzambi: Yes...Yes... I think it is fine...we'll do that.

Kuta: You think I'm crazy? It is a known tendency here in Nyakibonga: when you speak facts, they say you are crazy. As days goes by, all of you also will be crazy. *[Pointing at Nzambi, Debra and Mdeni.]* Fine we'll see.

Debra: I'm also informed that HIV/AIDS is a problem here in Nyakhibongah, so I have brought condoms with me and they will be distributed for free as well. This is to protect youth, our youth here. I really felt so sad when I heard most of you are HIV orphans. It painfully touched my heart. *[Nzambi nods.]*

Kuta: *[Furiously.]* We mjinga nini?[50] Do you mean, that we are the only ones who die of HIV? No wonder nowadays suckers have changed their approach. I say wait and see.

Voices are heard from back stage.

Mdeni: *[Enters Mdeni, terrified, whispers to Nzambi.]* Farmers and herders are fighting on the other side of the mountain. And they are saying, unless your Excellency Mr. Nzambi takes your time to go and listen, *hakutakalika.*[51]

Debra: *[Confidently.]* I think we need to put another project on this, Mr. Nzambi. We can establish something like the hanging gardens of Babylon, a place where these farmers can farm peacefully from above and cattle herders stay at the bottom in harmony. What do you think about this idea, Mr. Nzambi?

Ndanwa peeps again to give a signal to Nzambi to look into the pot. Nzambi ignores him and continues talking.

Nzambi: This is a great idea and we'll make a policy on it.

Kuta: *[Jokingly facing audience.]* We'll make policies even for beards and hair, wait and see!

---

50   Are you a fool or?

51   It will be chaos.

Nzambi: I'll also tell my people to endorse these projects, but if you have ready-made contracts with you here, we can sign. We've promised the best life for our people and we must deliver. The best life... *[Mdeni leads others to clap.]*

Kuta: *[Calling out.]* Wewe[52], all these problems have been brought by you *[Pointing at Debra.]* and those two people who you are sitting with. *[Pointing at Nzambi and Mdeni.]* Why don't you think of a project which can take you with your fellow narrow minded people to your home country? Actually, we don't need you. We, the great Nyakibongans have no problems. You are our problems!

Nzambi smiles, Debra is puzzled, while Mdeni stands.

Mdeni: Can you please wait for the question and answer session?

Kuta: Yes, I will...because I know you have ready-made answers.

Nzambi: I have a feeling that she belongs to the opposition. And these are the ones who are using her.

Enter people with machetes and stones, singing.

> Haya manyani yakifa
> Mimi siwezi kulia
> Nitayatupa Kagera
> Yawe chakula cha mamba
> Piga magoti we mwizi
> Piga magoti we mwewe
> Piga magoti we nyoka
> Kwa Wananyakibonga wote[53]

Man 1: Yes, there he is!

---

[52] You

[53] If these monkeys die / I won't cry / I'll throw them in Kagera / to be crocodiles' food / kneel down you thief / kneel down you hawk / kneel down you snake / to all Nyakibongas.

Man 2: No, he is not there!

Woman: They are all the same men and women, with the same behavior as if they all come from the same womb.

Man 1: [*Sharply.*] We must revenge her!

Mdeni: [*Softly.*] *Tafadhali tusikilizane.*[54]

Woman: With who? We cannot listen to traitors… My daughter is only 12 years old and they have … They have… [*She cries loudly.*] They have taken my *shamba*[55] and made it a mine… Now they have turned my daughter into a mine too and they take minerals from her… [*Continues to cry.*]

Man 2: I propose we look for men and not this ka-lady.

Man 1: We should not waste our time… We have to do the same… Take off your … I say take of your nanihii! …

Nzambi: [*Turning and grinning.*] Human rights … my people, this is against human rights!

Woman: Do the same to her as his fellows in the mines have done to my daughter.

Ndanwa peeps again to give a signal to Nzambi to keep quiet.

Nzambi: [*Slowly puts out his hands.*] We cannot attract investors if we behave like this. We must create a good environment for investment. This behaviour will tarnish our reputation.

Kuta: You mop head! Good environment… [*Laughing loudly.*] good environment even if it costs our lives; good environment… even if they enslave our people…; good environment…even if they take your wife [*Pointing at Nzambi.*]…; Good environment. Thank you, your honour!

Debra: [*Trembling and horrified.*] People of Nyakhibongah,

---

54 Please, let's listen to each other.

55 Farm

you should not blame us. How could we know we should bring water, mosquito nets and condoms in exchange for gold, tanzanite and now gas? For me I hardly know where Nyakhibongah is. *[Kuta smiles at Nzambi.]*

Scene 2

The stage is covered with a big banner written United Republic of Nyakibonga. Launching a Manicure and Pedicure National Campaign. Enters dancers dancing mkwajungoma.

> Nguvu zetu eeh…utamaduni
>
> Maisha yetu eeh…utamaduni
>
> Tudumishe eeh…utamaduni[56]

After a few minutes of dancing, Nzambi stands to take a group picture with the dancers. Ndanwa peeps to warn Nzambi for not looking into the pot. Nzambi seems not to bother.

Nzambi: *[To dancers.]* *Asanteni sana*[57]. I feel happy to see how we preserve our traditions. *Nyie ndio kioo cha jamii*[58]. As I promised in my campaigns, I have reserved a cake for you artists… Please keep on waiting. *[To the audience.]* Good people of Nyakibonga: today we are launching this manicure and pedicure campaign. As stated in our election manifesto, it is important for everyone here in Nyakibonga to have clean, polished and well decorated nails. *[The Officer brings a decorated box with a pair of scissors and places it in front of Nzambi. Nzambi takes the scissors and cuts it. He takes out a few nail clippers and shows them to the audience.]* This is what we call good life, better life, even the best life my government has promised. Later

---

[56] Our energy…culture / our life…culture / let's sustain…culture

[57] Thank you very much.

[58] You are the society's mirror.

my wife and I will go for a manicure and pedicure. As you know, we must preach what we practice.

Kuta: I wonder: Is this, what we have been promised? We'll see *maajabu*[59] in this business, I mean this political entrepreneurship.

Mdeni: Kuta, you seem to be thinking too deeply.

Kuta: We had, *Mtu ni Afya, Siasa ni Kilimo*[60] and the rest, why shouldn't we revive these campaigns?

Mdeni: I know you still believe as Mwalimu did. All of his bogus ideologies, including his famous *Ujamaa*[61] which he himself failed to make work, were so chaotic. We replaced them because they were not making sense in these IT years. By the way, *msiba wa masikini, mtaji wa tajiri!* [62] [*Whispering.*] You know His Excellency is a very hard working person. Currently he is working on an oxygen provision program for people living in the slums. He'll send his deputy to launch it next month as His Excellency, himself, will not be around; he'll be attending international matters.

Kuta: [*Looking at Mdeni with desperate eyes.*] Vasco da Gama of the 21st century…. Mdeni, are you a believer?

Mdeni: A believer? In what? *Ujamaa* or *Ubepari*[63]? Is this your question?

Kuta: Simple question: Mdeni are you a believer?

Mdeni: Yes, why not.

Kuta: Follow me! [*Four mdundiko drum beats are heard.*]

---

[59] Miracles

[60] Human is Health, Politics is Agriculture

[61] Tanzanian socialism.

[62] Poor person's mourning, rich person's capital.

[63] Capitalism

Scene 3

A mdundiko procession led by Mdeni, who now holds a big cooking pot.

> *Mdundiko waah!*
> *Tunapita tunapita,*
> *Mdundiko waah!*
> *Asiye na jiwe, aeleke mwana,*
> *Mdundiko waah!*
> *Kama huna gololi, weka macho,*
> *Mdundiko waah!*
> *Kama huna miguu, njoo na gari,*
> *Mdundiko waah!*[64]

Mdeni: I have not seen His Excellency, Mr. Nzambi. Does he have any information?

Kuta: To do what?

Mdeni: *Yeye ndiye mkuu wa kambi.*[65] He must be well informed.

Kuta: Yes and no. By the way, he has a strong intelligence; he must have received the news.

Mdeni: Are we allowed to demonstrate?

Kuta: We are not demonstrating; we are dancing. Is a dancing procession a demonstration? This is a traditional procession. We don't need dogs and horses to guide us. We are not like the world worrying terrorists.

Mdeni: But people are holding plackards and I have this briefcase.

Kuta: Yes, of course. This is one way of integrating IT in our traditions. The good thing about Nzambi is that he does

---

[64] Mdundiko waah / we are passing, we are passing / Mdundiko waah / if you don't have a stone, carry a child / Mdundiko waah / if you don't have marbles put eyes / Mdundiko waah / if you don't have legs come with the car / Mdundiko waah

[65] He is the head of the camp.

not care. The best he can offer on this issue is his endless smile.

Mdeni: I'm worried they'll arrest us.

Kuta: If they try, I'll tell them to their faces to start with the sworn-in professional witches of Nyakibonga who sit down there at our shrine, thinking from their stomachs! [*Kuta possessed; praying with nearly motionless lips.*] I, the owner of the land, the most honored, I knock on your doors, my grandparents. We have brought our sufferings, our pains, our tears; we need your blessings.

Mdeni: [*Calling out while terrified.*] Kuta…Kuta…Kuta! … Don't say it now. We are not yet there.

Kuta: [*Standing still, raising her hands.*] We know some of us are dirty, holding our offerings.

Mdeni: [*Drops the cooking pot while calling.*] Nzambi… Nzambi!…

Condoms, mosquito nets, dollars, cell phones, hair rollers, body creams and various reports and contracts get out of the cooking pot. Ndanwa peeps out and smiles to the audience.

Kuta: You can see them from their acts and not their words. They need to be cleaned. We need you to clean them.

Enters Ndanwa.

Ndanwa: Excuse me, why are you here?

Kuta: To give offerings and ask for forgiveness.

Ndanwa: [*Whispers to Kuta.*] Please tell Murungu the Great, to help Nzambi to see, instead of being shown.

Kuta: Murungu, the most honoured, we are bringing to your attention the sweat of the servants who are not sure of tomorrow. We are offering the tears of the unheard and the blood of the bloodsuckers.

Ndanwa: [*Whispering to Kuta.*] Yes, and also the minds of our unethical budgeters who cannot budget for themselves, but, always budget for us. Those who always neglect the womb where they came from, those who sit at the shrine to strike murderous deals for Nyakibonga, let them wake up! Clean their minds and hearts and protect the few from the majority of mischievous sprites! *Yaani uso usio na haya usiwaone!*[66]

Scene 4

Mdeni is still lying on the ground. The dancers come with mangaka dance.

> *Siku hii siku hii*
> *Ni ya furaha sana*
> *Tumshangilie mwenyekiti*
> *Kwani yeye ni mambo yote*[67]

Murungu: [*Murungu's voice is heard from backstage.*] How can you be cleaned, while you are not dirty?

Kuta: We are, your majesty; see our hands.

Murungu: [*Murungu's voice*] You are not…

The dirty ones are sitting on the other bank of the river, drinking your sweet sweat while blowing a whistle.

The dirty ones are the ones who must take a flight to take a shower and dry clean their clothes.

The dirty ones are the ones who never cry the way you cry.

The dirty ones are dancing sweet melodies on red carpets and not in the dust like you.

---

[66] I mean, an unprotected face should not see him.

[67] This day this day / is a happy day / we should praise the chairperson / because s/he is everything. This day this day / is a happy day / we should praise the chairperson / because s/he is everything.

The dirty ones are covering themselves with aduvet and not with animal skins.

The dirty ones are the ones who require being praised and blessed for their wrong doings.

Kuta: Mdeni…Mdeni!

Mdeni: Yes …is it you, Kuta? [*Mdeni looks around as if he is looking for something in vain.*]

Kuta: Yes, have you heard?

Mdeni: [*Gets up.*] Sijasikia[68]…I was not there.

Kuta: The almighty Murungu said she has no objection to our cleansing ritual. But the dirty ones have boycotted the ritual and organized their own.

Mdeni: No! No! No! Kuta, tell her, we are all here. We beg for His forgiveness. Tell her, we are forced to hug the wicked and push away the good. By the way, is she not the same Murungu to whom we pray for peace, rain, and good harvest?

Kuta: Yes.

Mdeni: I doubt it: she has been so bitter today. Ask her why she is furious.

Kuta: You remember Mdeni, this is the same Murungu we asked for support; we embarked on our *fagio la chuma* movement including the *wahujumu uchumi*[69] detention. How can we think corruption is a new phenomenon? By the way, we have used the wrong dance…

Mdeni: [*Terrified.*] So?

Kuta: We have to suffer the consequences!

Mdeni: [*Imploring.*] Kuta, please try your best… The time is now.

Murungu: (V/O) Are you sure you want to be cleaned?

---

[68] I haven't heard.

[69] Iron broom .. economic saboteurs

Mdeni: Yes.

Murungu: (V/O) Tell Nzambi to ask for forgiveness first. He has to be cleaned *alishiriki karamu chafu*[70]... Now his hands are dirty; that's why everything he touches becomes dirty.

Kuta: I knew... I know and I said you will see.

Mdeni: So who will clean the mop?

Scene 5

Lead by Ndanwa, they form a dance procession playing kibati.

> *Leo mtaona, leo mtaona!*
> *Leo mtasikia ya kusikia!*
> *Leo mtashuhudia kudondokea pua!*
> *Haki ya mungu asipoumbuka mtu, mie kibati sichezi tena![71]*

Mkarara: Thank you very much, our honorable soothsayers. As we are well aware, every research needs to provide its findings. For years we've been working on several hypotheses. We found out that there are more pertinent issues to address here in Nyakibonga than envisioned. On behalf of the research team, I would like to take this opportunity to welcome His Excellency Mr. Nzambi to officiate the findings.

Nzambi: My work here is very simple, just to read the findings. [*Kuta smiles.*] The findings are: if you don't clean the mop, it won't mop well. It will make the floor worse. So we clean the mop not because we love it, but rather we are avoiding the consequences of using a dirty mop.

---

[70] S/he participated in the dirty feast

[71] Today you'll see, today you'll see / Today you'll hear what to hear / Today you'll witness falling on nose / I swear if someone's reputation is not ruined / I won't play *kibati* again.

[*He smiles.*] Thank you for your attention and God bless Nyakibonga.

Ndanwa: [*To the audience.*] God bless Nyakibonga... God are these the promised saviors? Reading what they don't know... Reading what they don't even understand... Reading even rotten speeches.

Lead by Kuta, segere dancers blow the air.

Nilisema...nilisema
Nilisema ...nilisema
Tubebeshe...tubebeshe
Tubebeshe umaskini tufe nao
Maneno kidogo...ya Nyakibonga hayo[72]

---

[72] I said , I said / I said , I said / give us a burden , give us a burden / give us a poverty burden to die with / just a few words, from Nyakibonga

List of Contributors

Ms. Zuhura Badru studied Education (Literature and Kiswahili) at UDSM, graduating in 2008.

Mr. Benjamin Branoff studied at UDSM in 2006, as a semester abroad from the University of Florida.

Ms. Anna Chikoti studied Education (English) at UDSM, graduating in 2008.

Mr. Emmanuel Lema is a Teaching Assistant at UDSM, pursuing a Master's degree in Literature.

Ms. Kimberley McLeod studied at UDSM in 2008, as a semester abroad from Georgetown University.

Mr. Simon Mlundi studies Education (Literature and Foreign Languages) at UDSM, and will graduate in 2009.

Mr. Yunus Ng'umbi is a Teaching Assistant at UDSM, pursuing a Master's degree in Literature.

Dr. Lisa María Burgess Noudéhou is a Senior Lecturer in the Department of Literature at UDSM (Ph.D. UPENN).

Dr. Frowin Paul Nyoni is a Senior Lecturer in the Department of Fine and Performing Arts at UDSM (Ph.D. Leeds).

Dr. Lilian Osaki is a Senior Lecturer in the Department of Literature at UDSM (Ph.D. Florida).

Ms. Vicensia Shule is an Assistant Lecturer in the Department of Fine and Performing Arts at UDSM.

Prof. Saida Yahya-Othman is an Associate Professor in the Department of Foreign Languages at UDSM (Ph.D. UDSM).